Terminal Disaster

Inside the Money Machine

by
Randall Radic
and
Ralph Fontana

For information about special discounts for bulk purchases, please contact Sunbury Press, Inc. Wholesale Dept. at (717) 254-7274 or orders@sunburypress.com.

To request one of our authors for speaking engagements or book signings, please contact Sunbury Press, Inc. Publicity Dept. at publicity@sunburypress.com.

FIRST SUNBURY PRESS EDITION
Printed in the United States of America
February 2012

Trade Paperback ISBN: 978-1-62006-033-9
Mobipocket format (Kindle) ISBN: 978-1- 62006-034-6
ePub format (Nook) ISBN: 978-1-62006-035-3

Published by:
Sunbury Press
Camp Hill, PA
www.sunburypress.com

Camp Hill, Pennsylvania USA

Prologue

As a young officer stationed at Fort Benning, Georgia in 1969, I made a unique discovery that would have a lasting effect on me, and it took me years to realize it.

I went to my mailbox one afternoon, and in my mail was a letter from the Fourth National Bank of Columbus. For those "not in the know," Columbus, Georgia is the host city for Fort Benning, also known as "The Infantry Center." And yes, there was actually a bank with that name. I always wondered what happened to the First, Second, and Third National Bank of Columbus, but never found out. That is for another story.

In the envelope was a letter, as well as a plastic card called a "Master Charge," which I had never heard of. The letter explained to me that the Ft. Benning Officer's Club was canceling all of the current membership cards, and would be using the new Master Charge card as our official Officers Club card. Not only that, but we would no longer have to pay our bill in full each month like we were absolutely, positively required to do. No exceptions. And the reason was the Master Charge card was a "Credit Card"—not to be confused with the "Charge Cards" which I had. One of the first things I did when I received my commission, thanks to my father's advice (as well as him co-signing for me) was to get a Diners Club card and an American Express card. In the military, there are frequent transfers, travel, and other things that required some sort of credit since we only were paid once each month in those days.

In addition, in 1969, young officers were not exactly high wage earners. A second lieutenant's base pay was $288, and as a Captain at that time, I made slightly over $1,000 per-month. The per-month is important, because no matter what you did, and how you planned it, by the 25th of each month you were (or at least the vast majority of us) effectively "broke." So the verbiage in the letter was especially important.

It simply stated that not only could we use the card to charge our monthly dues, meals, beverages, and other things the club offered, but also we *did not have to pay in full each month*! We could make payments on our charges! We could eat and drink—even after the 25th! What a great idea!

Not wanting to make any unwarranted assumptions, and not truly believing this miracle had happened, I stopped by the bank on the way back to the post. I talked with a manager there, and he assured me that everything I read was true! Miracles do happen! In addition, he asked if I had a family and any children, and if I intended to stay in the Army. When I answered yes, he automatically increased my credit line by $500. So now I had a grand total of $1,000 available on my new Credit Card!

However, I mentioned to him that unless I bought drinks for all of my guys each night, took my family to eat every Saturday and Sunday, and drank myself into oblivion each month, I really didn't need the high credit line.

That's when he really got my attention. He explained to me that not only was it an Officers Club card, it was also a card that I could use to buy uniforms, plane tickets, flowers, and just about anything that I could imagine. When I asked him where I could shop and do all of these things, he said any merchant that had the sign "We Accept Master Charge" would accept the card. Wow! I am loving what I am hearing! I am only making $1,000 per month, and now I can use this card for other things, and not even have to pay for it in full each month like the Diners Card and American Express. Won't my wife be surprised!

And she was. So much so that when I told her of our good fortune, she promptly went up-and down Victory Drive (the main drag in Columbus) to see where she could use our newfound wealth. Bad move.

When I got home that night, she explained to me there were only seven stores that she found that accepted Master Charge. We were being tricked!

To stay out of trouble with the wife, and to not look like I was a complete rube, I called the manager the next day. He explained to me that they were actively marketing, and very, very soon there would be "hundreds" of merchants that accepted the card.

It was a great concept. First, set up the Officers Club to accept the card. Now, our dues would be charged automatically every month, and we could increase our spending at the club, and Master Charge would pay the club in full. No more embarrassing calls from the club manager about one of my young lieutenants being late. In those days, it was a Mortal Sin for any officer to have one of those types of calls or letters from anyone, let alone the Officers Club. They said it was a sign of "bad character" if such a letter or phone call was received. I always felt it was a sign of not being paid enough. The Lieutenant's pay was $288, and right off the top, he had to pay $30 in Club dues. And it was not an option to belong or not. You belonged! That left him or her with $250 for the rest of the month. Go figure.

So, there were *thousands* of cards sent to a relatively credit-worthy group of cardholders the same week in the same city. How hard would it be to have a sales force swamp the merchants in the area and tell them of this new gadget, and how their sales would *increase many times over* if they would just accept the card? This is a no-brainer, and was to set the stage for the next forty-plus years of "signing the merchant".

And it *did* happen just like the bank manger said. Except there were not hundreds but *thousands* of merchants in the next year that accepted not only Master Charge, but also another card called The Bank Americard.

Fast forward around fifteen years, and I was in the airplane business. One day, I received a phone call from my secretary in Atlanta that would change my life for the rest of my working days.

I was in Boston at the time working with one of our company's dealers. She explained to me that I should come home soon, like that day or the following day, since my immediate supervisor was fired, as well as myself and seven of my peers from across the country that reported to him. I had never been fired before, but I knew it was bad, bad, bad. It seems that our parent company, a large Fortune 50 company, had decided that the time was right to get rid of some middle managers. And they did it with the cold, cruel efficiency that only a large corporation can do. They boxed the contents of my desk, sealed it, and placed it at security for my return. What a way to go! When I took my little box home, I opened it to see what was left. They were excellent at acting like cold-hearted suits when they let us go, they were not very good at the filtering process, and left me with several important and proprietary items. The most important of those items was my Rolodex (remember those?)

Over the next few days, I pondered my future and decided to change careers. I was still relatively young, still had the energy that a successful sales and marketing guy should have, and wanted to try a new industry. And one of the first cards that I retrieved from my Rolodex was a card from a banker that we had sold some airplanes to. I called him, and he told me that there was a "new thing" in the credit card side of the business, and it involved something called a "credit card machine", and he thought that I would be great at it, and make ten times as much money as I made in the airplane business. I liked what he had to say, and he put me in touch with a contact in Atlanta.

My life changed with that phone call. Over the next twenty years, I was involved in marketing credit card processing agreements to merchants. *And terminals.* Very, very important to remember terminals. And during that time, I have witnessed, and more times than I wish to admit participated in, the "seedy" side of this industry. It is what I call a "hidden industry" because *almost no one* knows about it! Most merchants believe that the "bank" is the credit card processor, when in reality it is a sales force that feeds the oxygen of new merchants and thus new sales to Master Card and VISA. It is a sales force that, by and large, takes advantage of the merchant in any way that they can—and with the full acknowledgment of MC and VISA—sometimes with wink and a nod, and other times with full understanding of the underhanded, sleazy, and deceptive tactics and financial gimmickry that would impress Bernie Madoff. And it continues to this day; each and every day. Unknowing merchants are at the mercy of the rep either being honest, or being a true snake with larceny in his (or her) heart. Some of the most prolific practitioners of deceptive and misleading sales techniques are women.

Which brings me to the reason why I decided to write this book.

I have been in this industry for many, many years both in the front office, back office, as a bank executive, and owner of my own sales force which did many thousands of merchant agreements over the years. I like to say that there is nothing that I have not seen in this business. That is probably not 100% correct, but it is very close. I have seen both bankers and sales agents lie, cheat and steal, and use tactics purposefully designed to deceive and fleece the merchant.

So, the simple answer might be that I have my own axe to grind, and have also been deceived and cheated by some of the people I have worked with, and for.

But that is too simple. I decided that I would tell my story for a variety of reasons:

1. I think it's unknown.
2. I think it's entertaining.
3. I think I can help merchants stay out of trouble, *and save money,* if they know what is going on.
4. I think I can sell some books and earn some money since I will not be able to stay in this business in any way going forward.
5. I would love to really, truly irritate and anger some people.

If you are a merchant, or about to go into business, I ask that you read this book first and save yourself thousands of dollars and many, many headaches. When you have the history and the knowledge contained in my book, then you will have the tools, and more than a fighting chance, to save yourself money as well as many headaches and legal hassles that lurk in this shark-filled industry for the unknowing.

Chapter 1
Birth of an Industry

Frank X. McNamara was a moneylender. He had an office in the Empire State building, from which he ran his small, private loan company: Hamilton Credit Corporation. The term 'corporation' made it sound like it was a major enterprise. Really, it was just one step up from a loan-shark business, but it paid the bills and McNamara kept his eyes and ears open, looking for good business opportunities. Because that's what Frank McNamara was. He was an opportunist.

It was 1950. World War II was over and the U.S. economy was taking off. Everyone was hustling and, if you played your cards right, you could go places and be somebody. And that's what McNamara was doing, looking for an open door to the promised land of cash flow. He didn't want to be a day laborer, working for so much an hour. He wanted his money to work for him. That's why he went into the lending business. The way he figured it was by making small loans the interest would trickle back into his pocket at a nice steady rate. If he made enough small loans, the trickles would eventually form a river of money flowing his way.

It was called credit. And credit, in McNamara's opinion, was where the action was. The way people thought was changing. They didn't want to wait to buy the things they wanted. They wanted to gratify their desires right now. And that's where McNamara came in. He gave them credit. He loaned them the money to buy what they wanted. They paid him back by making monthly payments, including an interest charge. The interest charge was McNamara's profit.

It was simple and beautiful. Everybody was happy. McNamara was happy because his money worked for him. He didn't work for his money. And his debtors were happy because they got what they wanted – a new car, new clothes, nice furniture.

One of McNamara's best customers was a local businessman who came in once or twice a month and borrowed a moderate amount of money, which he paid back as regular as clockwork. Since the businessman appeared to be prosperous, McNamara wondered why the man required frequent loans. So one day, McNamara asked him.

The businessman told McNamara that he had a number of department-store charge accounts. A lot of his friends didn't have any charge accounts, because they couldn't qualify for them. Still, they wanted to buy things from the department stores. Only they didn't have enough money. In other words, they were between a rock and a hard place. They couldn't afford the items they wanted to buy, and the stores wouldn't give them any credit.

So the businessman loaned his department-store charge cards to his friends, and charged them a fee for the use of the card. Then he borrowed money from McNamara to pay off the cumulative charge card debts at the end of each month. The difference between the interest he paid to McNamara and the interest he charged his friends was his profit.

McNamara was impressed. The businessman had a good thing going. McNamara parked the information in the back of his brain and went about his business. Not long after, the businessman came in to make another loan. He told McNamara it would be his last.

"How come?" asked McNamara, hating to lose a steady customer.

"One of my customers skipped town," replied the businessman. "Which means I'm stuck with the debt he ran up on my charge card. I can't afford to take any more risks."

McNamara nodded. He understood. Delinquent debtors were a common problem. McNamara got around the problem by padding his interest rates. His rates were high enough to cover the inevitable losses that were part of the credit business. Things happened. Sometimes people were unable to pay their debts. Smart guys knew this, allowed for it, and protected themselves. Smart guys spread the risk factor out to their customers.

Later the same day, McNamara was having lunch with his attorney, Ralph Schneider. The topic of discussion was how to recover an outstanding debt that McNamara found himself stuck holding. As the men ate, they talked about the different methods of legal recourse available.

McNamara stopped and sat motionless. Out of nowhere, a thought blossomed in his head. It was an idea of pure genius. A single charge plate usable at lots of different establishments. Instead of each store issuing a proprietary charge plate, which could be used only at one store, there would be one charge plate good at many stores.

Glancing around at the restaurant in which he was seated, Major's Cabin Grill, McNamara realized that restaurants were the perfect candidates for his idea. Excited, he interrupted Schneider, who was babbling about litigation.

"Listen to this!" said McNamara, leaning forward. He proceeded to outline his grand idea.

Schneider liked what he heard. After asking a few questions, he told McNamara that he wanted in. He was willing to put up $15,000.

McNamara put up $25,000, which was a lot of money in 1950. They found another investor, Matty Simmons, who, once they explained the idea, was gung-ho.

McNamara leased a three-room office in the Empire State Building. The three men went from restaurant to restaurant in New York, explaining the advantages of their concept to the restaurateurs. A few months later, they had signed up twenty-two restaurants and one hotel.

On February 8, 1950, McNamara, Schneider and Simmons dined at Major's Cabin Grill. McNamara paid for the meal with a brand new charge plate. The name on the plate was Diners Club.

In its first year of business, Diners Club didn't make a dime. In fact, it lost $58,000. But the idea caught on. More and more restaurants and hotels signed up. They couldn't afford not to participate, not if they wanted to remain competitive. By the end of its second year, Diners Club had revenue of $6 million, reporting a profit of $60,000.

The credit card industry was born.

One Thing Leads to Another

One year later, in 1951, the Franklin National Bank of New York came out with a multipurpose credit card for retail stores. Meanwhile, out in California, Bank of America issued its own multipurpose credit card. Across the country, other banks jumped on the credit card bandwagon, issuing cards locally to their best customers.

Then, in 1958, American Express tossed their hat into the ring. They came out with what came to be known as a travel and entertainment credit card, which was good at hotels, motels and restaurants.

Within a very short time, most of the banks with credit card programs were kicking themselves, wondering why they had ever gone into this crazy business. Their credit cards were losing them millions of dollars per year. The problem was the cost. Banks had to purchase expensive equipment, hire new people, and set up previously non-existent communication systems. Added to those expenditures were the advertising and marketing programs responsible for selling the credit card concept to the general public. If people didn't buy into the idea of using credit cards, then the merchants wouldn't sign on. And if the merchants didn't sign on, there would be no place for the public to use the cards. So the banks spent heavily, promoting their credit cards.

By 1965, it started to pay off. In California, Bank of America's BankAmericard was making money, and a lot of it. When the other banks recognized just how profitable an efficiently managed credit card operation could be, they all got greedy and jumped in feet first. Unfortunately, some of them forgot to look before they jumped. Instead of landing in the deep, luxurious waters of profitability, they plunged into the shallows and almost broke themselves.

In Chicago, First National Bank came out with the 'First' card. Across the street, Continental Bank issued a credit card called 'Town and Country.' And 'Charge It' was the name of Harris's card. All together, the banks of

Chicago "put on the air" (mailed out) over five million credit cards to anyone and everyone. It was a credit card free-for-all. Due diligence was fugitive. Credit worthiness was not even considered. Credit cards bearing the names of children and dead people arrived in mailboxes. Some people received as many as ten credit cards.

Many people thought of the credit cards, a newfangled idea, as free money. They went on extravagant spending sprees, paying for their goods with their new cards. "Charge it" became the new mantra. Everyone forgot that sooner or later the Piper had to be paid.

Merchants were ecstatic. They turned vast piles of drafts into the banks and demanded immediate payment. The banks paid.

Of course, fraud was everywhere. People used cards that didn't belong to them or that they had found or that someone had sold them for a nominal fee. Who wouldn't pay $100 dollars for a card that could be used to purchase $500 worth of items? Mail thieves plucked cards out of mailboxes, signed the back of the card and went shopping.

The banks paid.

Similar scenarios took place all over the country. The banks had no one to blame but themselves. They had bought mailing lists of people without checking financial backgrounds. Compounding the problem were unprotected mailings, lost cards, fraud, theft, and non-payment. It was a disaster. Millions of dollars were lost through disorganization and negligence.

There was a bigger problem. The credit cards were not universally accepted. They were limited to the area served by the issuing bank. In many cities, this meant the card was good only in that city. Even Bank of America's BankAmericard was limited to the state of California, which had branch banking. Faced with this dilemma, some of the smarter bankers in Illinois got together and formed a regional organization, which honored member banks' credit cards. They called it the Midwest Bank Card. The group published a 'hot-card' list that member merchants could use to detect fraud.

The Midwest Bank Card was a good idea. For it expanded the card's acceptance from a local sphere to a regional sphere. However, there were still limitations. It wasn't enough.

The stage was now set for a national bank card.

Kenneth Larkin, who was one of the smartest guys at California's Bank of America, realized what needed to be done. So he did it. On March 25, 1966, he sent a memo to the directors of the bank. In his memo, Larkin set forth a whale of an idea. To wit, that BankAmericard go nationwide. Bank of America would license member banks to use the name, the format, the program, and the systems of BankAmericard. The directors bought the proposal. They directed Larkin to set the wheels in motion.

Meanwhile, four other California banks—The Bank of California, Crocker-Citizens National Bank, United California Bank, and Wells Fargo—agreed that a national bank card was a wonderful idea. Only they didn't like the part about Bank of America running the show. So they decided to come up with their own national bank card. The foursome called their organization the California Bankcard Association. And it was a big hit. Many banks in California signed on, as did banks in Idaho, Nevada, Oregon, Washington, Utah, and Wyoming. And because many of its member banks were outside of California, a short time later the name of the association changed. It became known as the Western States Bankcard Association.

At almost the same time, a group of banks on the other side of the country had come up with their own idea for a national bank card. Banks in Pittsburgh, Virginia and Washington D.C. established the Interbank Card Association. Naturally, their card was to be called the Interbank Card.

The California Bankcard Association (soon to be called Western States Bankcard Association) heard about the Interbank Card and thought it sounded like a winner. They asked for permission to use "Interbank Card" on their cards, which were going to be called "Master Charge." Permission would automatically open the door to a national affiliation. The Interbank Card Association agreed.

At first, all the member banks of Interbank issued their own cards. None of the cards looked the same. There were different colors, different logos and different names on the cards. A small "i" in the corner of the cards was the only thing demonstrating their participation in a national bank card system.

Interbank's competitor, the members of BankAmericard, enjoyed the advantage of uniform appearance. The cards had the same name and same look. All the cards were blue, white and gold. This meant the BankAmericard carried more brand identification, which explained why, by 1968, BankAmericard had 16.7 million cardholders and 400,000 merchants to Interbank's 6 million cardholders and 150,000 merchants.

As far as Interbank was concerned, being number two was unacceptable. So they decided to establish their own brand. Borrowing the name Master Charge from its California members, they designed a white card with red and yellow circles for all their member banks. No more hodgepodge colors and names. There was one card with one look and one name.

Even though BankAmericard and Master Charge dominated the credit card horizon, there still remained some holdouts. These holdouts had seen the handwriting on the wall. They knew they had to choose up sides, but they took their sweet time doing it. The Eastern States Bankcard Association, which included three gigantic banks —New York's Chemical Bank, Manufacturers Hanover Trust, and Marine Midland—finally chose Master Charge. The next to choose up sides was First National City Bank, which at that time was the third largest bank in the U.S. First National City Bank later came to be known as Citibank. They had been happy with their own card; called the "Everything" card, which boasted 1.3 million members. But they knew that if they wanted to be players, they needed to go national. So they adopted the attitude of "if you can't beat 'em, join 'cm." In the end, they joined up with Master Charge.

Which side a bank ultimately chose was important, because Master Charge and BankAmericard were as different as night and day. Master Charge was similar to ancient Greece in the way it operated. It was a true democracy composed of regional associations. There was no single governing entity. In other words, Master Charge was run by committees, which meant there was a lot of leeway in how things were done. This meant there weren't a lot of rules. Each member bank was allowed to establish its own credit card procedures and policies.

BankAmericard operated more like the Soviet Union under the dictatorship of Joe Stalin. There was no leeway at all. In fact, it was their way or hit the highway. Bank of America demanded that licensed bank members adhere to their rules, regulations, and fee structures. At Bank of America efficiency and discipline were the watchwords. Bank of America ran BankAmericard like a well-oiled machine.

After a while, Bank of America's strict policies started to rub some of their member banks the wrong way. Some member banks simply didn't agree with certain rules, which were incompatible with their financial operations. Other member banks had improved upon Bank of America's system. Using advanced technology and streamlined procedures, they were leaving Bank of America in the dust. They felt Bank of America needed to update its credit card operations. The single biggest complaint voiced by member banks concerned Bank of America's fee structure, which the banks considered excessive. Another problem, the second biggest complaint, was with the 'add-on' charges Bank of America kept coming up with.

When the member banks asked Bank of America to review and revise the policies, Bank of America played deaf. They didn't listen because they didn't want to hear it. Because of this obstinate attitude, Bank of America soon found itself facing a mutiny. Member banks threatened to leave BankAmericard. They would defect to Master Charge. There were even a few banks that hinted at antitrust lawsuits against Bank of America.

Bank of America's finely tuned well-oiled machine was about to seize up. So they did the only thing they could do: they gave in. This surrender gave birth to National BankAmericard Incorporated (NBI), which was a member-owned organization run by a board of directors. The licensing system was dropped and replaced by charter memberships in NBI.

VISA

The first president of National BankAmericard Incorporated, Dee Hock, was a banker from Seattle. A slender man, who wore glasses, Hock was smart, determined and blessed with a vision. Hock's vision was that the potential for credit cards was infinite. In other words, the potential for profit from credit cards was utterly immense. His vision, for better or worse, changed the credit card industry.

While the 3,000 member banks of NBI accustomed themselves to a new way of operating, Master Charge was forging ahead. They established thirteen computer centers across the U.S. These centers processed the interchange of sales slips, sorting out who owed how much to whom, along with providing an anti-fraud system that alerted merchants to suspicious credit cards.

By 1975, Master Charge had 37 million people using their card, along with 1.2 million merchants signed up. BankAmericard had signed up 1.2 million merchants and had 31.1 million card carriers. Both operations were making handsome profits.

Then the improbable happened. A single bank decided it didn't like the rules of the game. It was tired of being told what it could do and what it couldn't do.

The Worthen Bank, which was located in Little Rock, Arkansas, filed an anti-trust lawsuit against NBI. The Worthen Bank maintained that being forced to choose either Master Charge or BankAmericard was trade restraint. Worthen declared it should be allowed to issue and process both cards. The result was that everyone lawyered up and the legal battle began. After years of arguments and counter-arguments, and millions of dollars in legal fees, NBI gave in. It allowed its members to issue both Master Charge and BankAmericard credit cards. This concession was called 'duality.'

Some industry insiders suggested that Hock had manipulated the situation to NBI's advantage. Hock recognized that more banks issued Master Charge than BankAmericard. By permitting duality, Hock realized that NBI and BankAmericard could only improve its position.

Duality would alter the complexion of the competitive market for credit cards among banks. Prior to duality, it had been Master Charge against BankAmericard. Now it was every bank against every other bank, because there were no restrictions.

NBI, due to Hock's astuteness, began allowing organizations that were not banks to issue credit cards. Ultimately, these organizations functioned as an ad hoc sales force for BankAmericard. They signed up thousands upon thousands of merchants. And each merchant that signed on paid interchange fees, which put more money in BankAmericard's pockets.

Additionally, in an effort to bolster his numbers even more, Hock decided BankAmericard needed better and more focused advertising. The search for an appropriate advertising agency began. BankAmericard ran a 'beauty contest.' All the contestants gave it their best shot, and were either eliminated or moved on to the final stage of the contest.

As the beauty finalists paraded through, Hock and his fellow-directors didn't like any of the presentations. Finally, a small agency from San Francisco made its sales pitch, which consisted of simply changing the name of BankAmericard to Visa. The word 'Visa', it was explained, carried the same meaning throughout the entire world. Visa connoted travel, an open door, and a passport to the new and exciting.

Hock had his winner. NBI spent $10 million dollars over the next six-months announcing its new name. The first ad was absolute genius. It said, "We're keeping up with you." In other words, even though the world is changing at the speed of light, Visa will always be there. Visa will stand by you.

In 1980, Master Charge, taking a cue from Visa, decided to change its name as well. Master Charge became MasterCard. Although it was a small change, it had big psychological implications. For the word 'charge' indicated a debt was being incurred. And debts had to be repaid. Whereas the term MasterCard insinuated a sense of freedom: mastery over any situation. It dispelled any notion of repayment ever taking place. The term

MasterCard was designed to encourage unconstrained, spontaneous use of the card.

Up to this point in time, credit card transactions were hampered by technology. Before a credit card could be used, the transaction would have to be authorized over a telephone line. Once authorization was received, merchants used an imprinting machine, called a knuckle buster, to capture data from the credit card. Then the merchants manually completed a sales draft for each transaction. The entire process could take 5 to 15 minutes. At the end of each business day, the merchants would physically deposit the paper drafts at their bank, just like a check. The merchants would eventually receive credit for the deposits. But it could take a few days.

Each merchant was charged a fee, called an interchange fee, for each transaction. Under this knuckle buster system the fee structure was simple: a fixed amount was paid for each sales draft. Interchange fees ranged from 3.5% to 10% of each transaction. Since millions of transactions occurred each day, the fees derived from those transactions constituted billions of dollars.

The lion's share of the interchange fees went to MasterCard or Visa, not to the member banks. In other words, MasterCard and Visa had a nice little arrangement going. They were making money hand over fist. It was cash-flow-City.

Everything changed in 1984. The credit card industry mutated overnight. The floodgates opened. Even more money began to flow in.

Money has a way of bringing out the cheats and crooks.

Chapter 2
The Opening of the Floodgates

Rise of the Machines

Technology changed the credit card industry. Overnight, the industry was reinvented. For those involved, it was if they were transported from a small wheat farm in Kansas to a neon-lit nightclub in Los Angeles. Like Dorothy in *The Wizard of Oz* or Alice in *Through the Looking Glass*, they found themselves part of something new and incredible.

The something new and incredible was a terminal, an electronic card reading device that would electronically authorize the card. It was called the ZON terminal; also known as ZON Junior. First released in 1984, it was built by VeriFone, whose name reflected the machines they made: *Veri*fication teleph*one*. VeriFone was founded in Hawaii by William 'Bill' Melton in 1981.

This point of sale credit card terminal was the beginning of the electronic payment industry. In a New York minute, the manual system of capturing credit card data was extinct. The knuckle busters went the way of the dinosaurs. Electronic draft capture was the wave of the future and everyone knew it, especially the merchants. The terminal would not only save the merchants time, it would increase profits.

The newfangled terminals not only changed the way merchants did business they also changed the business of doing business. For another idea rode in on the coattails of the terminals: entrepreneurs. The companies these entrepreneurs started were called ISOs: independent sales organizations. The independent sales organizations didn't work for the banks and they didn't work for the credit card associations. They worked for themselves. They were independent third-party providers.

They were middlemen. And they came into existence because, as entrepreneurs, they saw a niche open up and they filled it. Prior to 1984 and electronic draft capture, if a merchant wanted to accept credit cards, he went to his bank and filled out an application. The bank would process the application. Part of the process included investigating the merchant's credit worthiness. How long had he been in business? What did his profit-loss statement look like? Was he reliable? And most importantly, did he pay his debts on time? More often than not, the process took about a month to complete. If the merchant passed, after 30 days he was signed up and received his knuckle buster. He could now accept credit cards at his place of business.

Many merchants elected not to accept credit cards. Really, it wasn't any faster than checks, because it still involved manually filling out a draft, which was then deposited at the bank, just like a check. And most customers still carried their checkbooks with them while shopping. So if a merchant didn't accept credit cards, it wasn't a big deal. The customer would simply write a check.

With the advent of credit card terminals, this type of thinking was about to change. The banks realized that merchants, whether they knew it or not and whether they liked it or not, would soon be forced to jump aboard the credit card ship. If merchants wanted to keep up with their competitors, they would need a terminal. The banks, of course, were excited about electronic draft capture. For it meant they could reduce the ocean of paper they had to deal with everyday. Plus, the banks could still charge a processing fee for each transaction. In fact, the way the banks figured it, they would be killing two birds with one terminal. No more paper checks and more transaction fees. It was simple math: more terminals equaled more fees, which meant greater profits for the banks.

There was one problem. To make more profit, the banks needed to get the terminals in the hands of the merchants fast. For the banks, it was a labor and time issue. Someone needed to articulate the value of electronic payment processing to prospective merchants. In other words, someone needed to sell the merchants on the idea of terminals. Unless the banks hired and deployed their own sales forces, it would not happen fast enough. Yet the cost associated with hiring a private sales force would effectively negate the banks' profit margin. The banks were stymied. They didn't know what to do.

But they did know that every second lost was money lost.

There was a niche to be filled. Entrepreneurs saw it, along with the banks. It was the opportunity for independent sales organizations to sell merchant services. The entrepreneurs came up with a simple plan. They would open small sales offices across the U.S. Each office would assemble an aggressive sales force with an eye on profitability. The sales agents (ISOs) would lease terminals to merchants. Leases would contain a profit margin for the ISOs, which would pay its salesmen a commission.

Success was imminent. Everyone concerned would be happy. The merchants would be happy because they could offer a convenient service to their customers. This service would translate into increased sales and profits. The banks would be happy because of reduced mountains of paperwork. And they would make money from transaction fees. The ISOs would make money off the terminal leases, which would make them happy. And if the ISOs were good, they could expand and begin operating on regional and national levels, which translated to even more money.

It was a win-win situation. Or so it seemed.

There was a teeny-weeny itsy-bitsy little problem. Just as in the Garden of Eden, paradise couldn't exist without a serpent. The term 'independent' in independent sales organization wasn't a mistake. Some of the entrepreneurs, the ISOs, were self-styled cowboys. They operated in their own distinctive way.

Not only was James R. Elliot a cowboy, he was also a genius. Of Irish-Catholic descent, Elliot had a colorful personality and vast quantities of charisma. He cursed like a sailor, yet displayed a magical touch when it came to recruiting, training and motivating people who worked for him.

At the same time VeriFone was introducing the ZON credit card processing terminal, Elliot lived and worked in

Westchester, Illinois, where he was a major player in real estate. A smooth operator, Elliot had a knack for matching the right buyer with the right seller. Described as a "real estate whiz" by some, he occasionally took risks that, in hindsight, proved to be precarious. But that was part of Elliot's magnetism. He was a gambler by nature.

The odds caught up with him in 1984. Convicted of mail fraud, he was sentenced to three months in jail and five years of probation. Apparently, Elliot had defrauded two federal G.I. Loan programs out of $135,000. A year and a half later, he pled guilty to another count of mail and wire fraud. In that instance, Elliot had received a series of loans from an Illinois savings and loan bank. The conflict arose from the fact that Elliot was a director of the bank. Sentenced to six months in jail, and four and a half years of probation, Elliot did his time and moved on.[1]

Another of Elliot's talents was his ability to perceive trends and their attendant opportunities. When Elliot first heard about VeriFone and the ZON terminal, it was as if he'd received a vision from God. The short-term and long-term potential of electronic payment processing stood out like the proverbial handwriting on the wall.

Elliot became a pioneer of independent sales organizations. Not only did he lead the way into the Promised Land of ISOs, Elliot also founded and ran the foremost ISO in the country.

Traveling to North Dakota, Elliot pitched his idea to a group of bankers. Essentially, Elliot's idea went like this: he would establish an independent sales organization, which would represent the banking alliance. The ISO would sell the services of the bank/processor alliance to merchants, offering the merchants a working system. In return, the ISO would be allowed to sign up merchants. Signing up a merchant involved providing the merchant with two things he had to have: a merchant account with a bank and a terminal. Without these two items the merchant could not accept credit cards.

---

1 'Phone Company Banned From State for 2 Years," *L.A. Times*, September 7, 1996.

According to Elliot's proposed plan, first the ISO would sign the merchants up for a merchant account. At the same time, the ISO would lease terminals to the merchants. By marking up the leasing fees, the ISO would make a profit. The banks would make their profit by charging merchants a fee, called a 'discount rate', for each transaction that passed through the merchant's account.

The North Dakota bankers listened attentively. After Elliot finished his pitch, the bankers thought about it. They liked it. To paraphrase the Bible, they "saw that it was good." It was good because it didn't cost them a dime. *It was like free money!*

The North Dakota bankers told Elliot to go for it.

Elliot did just that. He and his right hand man, Dave Giangreco, started a company called Peachtree Bankcard. Initially, Peachtree was one small office in Chicago. But with Elliot at the helm, in no time at all, Peachtree had offices all over the United States. In the end, Peachtree had established offices in most major cities.

Peachtree's sales reps worked on commission. The equation was simple: more merchants meant higher commissions. So "feet on the street" was the motto. Sales reps at each office blanketed the surrounding area as rapidly as they could. It wasn't difficult to sell merchants on the financial benefits of electronic payment processing. Peachtree's sales reps were signing up merchants 12 to 16 hours per day.

Elliot, ever the innovator, kept his sales reps motivated by paying on a daily basis. If a sales rep signed up and leased terminals to ten merchants on one day, he was paid his commission the next day. Elliot's policy was the perfect example of immediate gratification. His sales force didn't have to wait until the end of the month for their money. Getting paid everyday kept Peachtree's reps hungry for more. They not only competed with each other but with themselves. Each sales rep tried to sell more today than he had sold yesterday. A good sales rep made $10,000 to $15,000 per week.

At that time, the late 1980's and early 1990's, the credit card industry resembled the Wild, Wild West. There were no hard and fast rules. The ISOs were unregulated and followed no guidelines. The lack of stringent rules meant it was a numbers game. The game went like this. Whoever signs up the most merchants and leases the most terminals makes the most money. Even the banks and the credit card associations, Visa and MasterCard, got caught up in the fever of the game. More merchants translated to more fees, which translated to more profits.

According to some industry insiders, more profits meant the banks and Visa and MasterCard looked the other way. Supposedly, they knew what was going on, but pretended otherwise. They didn't want to shoot the goose that was laying the golden egg.

For the ISOs the golden egg was the lease. Among the reps it was called the "sizzle" of the lease. It worked like this: the ISO rep would approach the merchant, who was still processing credit cards the old-fashioned way (batch capture and bank deposit), telling the merchant he could save money on his discount fees. This got the merchant's attention. Merchants were very interested in saving money on discount fees, because it meant money in their pockets.

The first thing the ISO rep always did was to analyze the merchant's credit card sales. For the volume of credit card sales determined how much money the rep could save the merchant. And the amount saved determined the lease payment. The higher the savings, the higher the rep adjusted the lease payment. For example, if the rep could save the merchant $300 per month, the lease payment would be set at $139 per month. If the amount saved was only $100 per month, the rep would set the lease payment at $59 or $69 per month. In other words, the lease payment was driven by the amount the rep could show the merchant he could save.

There was no standard lease fee. The fee varied from merchant to merchant. And the vast majority of merchants never considered the total cost of the lease over 48 months. It wasn't $4,800. It was only $99 per month. The ISO reps knew this. It was human nature to think short-term. So the reps never mentioned the total debt the merchant was incurring. It was also human nature to be impressed by large sums of money, especially if it was money saved.

Knowing this, the reps always emphasized the merchants' savings in yearly terms.

The rep's sales pitch would go something like this: "Mr. Merchant, if you would allow us the opportunity to handle your processing, we can save you over $3,000 per year. And guess what? That's over $12,000 in four years. And that's a lot of money. Just think of what you could do with $12,000 you didn't even know you had."

That was the beauty of lease payments, merchants rarely objected to the amount, if they thought they were saving money. And they were saving money. What the merchants didn't know was that the savings were arbitrary. The amount merchants' saved was subject to the rep's judgment of how much the merchants could afford to pay.

There was another factor the merchants were ignorant of. The manner in which ISOs paid their reps greatly influenced the merchants' lease payments. An average 48-month lease of $99 per month resulted in the merchant paying $4,752 over the life of the lease. Of that total, $3,045 went to the ISO straight from the leasing company. The company would pay the sales rep his portion (usually between 50 to 75%) of the $2,700, in cash money, the day after the merchant signed the lease. Sales reps never had to wait 48 months for their commission. They got their commission right now.

In the framework of that scenario, the incentive to keep the merchants' fee as low as possible was non-existent. High lease fees translated into higher commissions. Higher commissions became the true incentive.

The "sizzle" of the lease.

All these factors, potential profits, the game of 'more,' the lack of rules, and the Wild, Wild West atmosphere, meant that the ISOs attracted a lot of cowboys, mavericks, and even some rogue cowboys. The primary interest of the rogues was money. Which meant they provided crappy service and charged high fees. It also meant the ISOs slacked off when it came to checking up on the credit worthiness of potential merchants. The sales reps simply signed the merchants up and leased them terminals. If a small percentage of the merchants didn't pay, it was no big deal. Because for every two that didn't pay, there were 98 new ones that did. It was all about the numbers.

The numbers were good. The sales reps couldn't sign merchants up fast enough.

There was more to it than that though. For merchants that didn't pay, there was a penalty. And it was serious. The ISOs had what was called the 'terminated merchant file' (TMF). If a merchant failed in his obligations, his name was placed on the TMF. The TMF was circulated nationally. Once a merchant's name appeared on the TMF, the merchant was blackballed. The merchant could never ever re-apply for a merchant account or a terminal. In other words, miscreant merchants were cut off at the financial knees. They were prohibited from ever accepting credit cards.

The terminated merchant file was a very effective form of punishment. For the merchants were made aware of its existence. The result was that most merchants paid.

Unfortunately, since the merchants were at the bottom of the food chain, some of the rogue sales reps took advantage of them. Outlandish scams took place.

The electronic card-reading terminal sold for $300. An honest sales rep leased the terminal to a merchant for $99 per month. The length of the standard lease was 48 months. Over the course of a 48-month lease the merchant ended up paying $4,752 for a $300 machine. Rogue reps leased the same machine to merchants for hundreds of dollars per month. And if the merchant only wanted to sign an 18-month lease, the rogues would take the lease agreement back to the office, where they changed the 1 to a 4. It was now a 48-month lease. And that's what the rogue sales rep was paid for. His commission was based on the agreement in hand.

The rogue sales reps were making out like bandits. There were rules, those established by the ISOs, but they never seemed to be enforced, so there were no repercussions. Essentially, it was legalized thievery. Everyone in the industry knew it was going on, but everyone chose to look the other way.

The merchant found out about the ruse 18-months later, when it was too late. And many times, the merchants never caught on. They just kept paying through the nose.

Peachtree Bankcard's sales force was responsible for a lot of such rip-offs. If Elliot was aware of it, and how could he not be? He shrugged it off. He was an entrepreneur, which meant he assumed the risk for the sake of profit. If there was no profit, then Elliot was responsible for the loss. That was what an entrepreneur did; he took the financial responsibility. ISOs were totally new. To Elliot's way of thinking, anytime a new business venture began errors and misjudgments occurred until the venture became firmly established. As far as Elliot was concerned, the thrill of being an entrepreneur was bound up in the unruliness and unpredictability of a new business. Anything could happen and usually did. That was what made it fun.

That being said, like any general, Elliot was ultimately responsible for the actions of his troops. And for a while, Elliot's troops ran wild. Peachtree Bankcard was making money hand over fist. The company was opening new offices daily, and soon had well over 100 across the U.S. Things were going great.

In fact, things were going too great. ISOs were unregulated and un-policed. In 1989, Visa and MasterCard, cognizant of what was going on, decided the ISOs were out of control. There were too many reports of flagrant abuse. Thus the card associations, Visa and MasterCard, instituted a number of ISO regulations and policies. Ostensibly, the card associations were demonstrating that they could police themselves. In reality, it was nothing more than lip service. A sham show of slapping miscreant ISOs on the wrist.

Industry insiders insinuated the regulations and policies were aimed directly at Peachtree Bankcard. *The Green Sheet*, which purported to be an industry magazine, but was little more than a scandal rag, suggested in its April 7, 1989 issue that Visa/MasterCard's new regulations were the result of "a certain player in the industry." That player, of course, was Jim Elliot and Peachtree. Shortly thereafter, Peachtree Bankcard sued

The Green Sheet for defamatory and libelous remarks. Nothing came of the lawsuit, as Peachtree Bankcard was merely posturing for effect. However, the lawsuit did set a precedent. Thereafter, on a regular basis, for a variety of reasons, *The Green Sheet* was sued.

Then in 1991, an investment firm from Manhattan, New York made Elliot an offer he couldn't refuse. The firm's name was Harbridge. Harbridge had noticed Peachtree and how much money it was making. By this time, there were hundreds of independent sales organizations. Everyone wanted a piece of the action. Harbridge wanted in too. But they wanted to start at the top, not at the bottom. So they contacted Elliot and asked if he was interested in selling.

Elliot said yes. A deal was struck. Harbridge Investments handed over a significant amount of money. Since Peachtree was a privately owned company, exactly how much money changed hands remains unknown. Educated guesses estimated somewhere between $100 and $200 million dollars.

Elliot took his money and did two things: one, he started another independent sales organization, calling it Cherry Payment Systems. The company's headquarters were in Downers Grove, Illinois. The second thing Elliot did reflected the primary reason he had sold Peachtree Bankcard. Elliot wanted his criminal record wiped clean. His felony convictions followed him wherever he went. It was as if he pulled a big black cloud along behind him. Not only was it annoying, it was also embarrassing. It was annoying because it limited his business options. Technically, a convicted felon was prohibited from performing certain fiduciary functions, such as representing the banking industry as an independent sales organization. He'd gotten away with it so far because he was darn good at what he did. So the banks and MasterCard looked the other way. But Elliot knew that sooner or later, like an 800-pound gorilla hiding in the kitchen pantry, his record would jump out and ruin the party.

More significantly his criminal record, on a personal level, embarrassed Elliot. To his way of thinking, he had done nothing illegal. He was not a criminal. He was an entrepreneur, which meant he took risks. And sometimes, to the untrained observer, those risks appeared to fall on the wrong side of the line. But in reality, they weren't illegal. They were daring gambles. And there was a vast difference between breaking the law and a risky financial venture.

So Elliot hired an attorney. The attorney's job was to expunge Elliot's criminal record. To perform this delicate legal operation, Elliot didn't hire just anybody. He wanted the best. Someone who knew how the system worked and what needed to done and who to contact to get it done. That someone was James R. Thompson, former governor of the state of Illinois. From 1977 to 1991, Thompson, who was known as 'Big Jim', had run the Illinois political machine. After stepping down as governor, Thompson became a partner at Winston and Strawn, attorneys at law. The law firm of Winston and Strawn was the crème de la crème of Illinois law firms.

Elliot visited Winston and Strawn, where he met with Thompson. Elliot explained what he wanted done. After listening, Thompson explained the situation to Elliot. There were two things Elliot needed to be very aware of: for one, it was possible to clean up his criminal record. However, there were no guarantees. It was a process that took time and patience. And the process could break down. For two, it would cost a lot of money.

Elliot understood. He had a lot of money and he had an intimate relationship with the concept of risk. He was prepared to pay.

Thompson took the case and went to work.

Meanwhile, Elliot changed the name of Cherry Payment Systems to Cherry Communications Incorporated. Cherry was expanding its operations to include pay phones and long-distance telephone service. Elliot and his buddy Dave Giangreco saw an opportunity. There was money to be made in communications.

At the time of the expansion, Cherry Payment Systems was chugging along as an independent sales organization, representing a number of banks, one of which was First Interstate Bank of South Dakota. Denny Sanford was the honcho at First Interstate. Sanford, well connected politically, was sponsoring a 1992 GOP dinner. Called the "President's Dinner," it was a fund-raiser for George Bush, Sr.

Somehow, Elliot became involved. No one recalled exactly how, but some industry insiders suggested the story went like this:

Sanford wanted to fill the banquet hall with high rollers. The price of admission was a hefty donation. Sanford needed someone with certain specialized skills to ensure this happened. He knew just the guy - James Elliot. Sanford directed Elliot to oversee the "President's Dinner."

Another version of the story implied Sanford wasn't directly involved. Instead, Allen Boyd, the president of Sanford's operation, may have recruited Elliot to ensure the event enjoyed a maximum turn out. Suffice to say Elliot became embroiled in the "President's Dinner." And apparently, Elliot elected not to leave anything to chance. The dinner would be chock-full of attendees.

Elliot informed the office managers of Cherry Payment Systems/Cherry Communications that each office would be collecting sizable donations from employees, who were 'encouraged' to attend the dinner. All the managers, who knew an order when they heard one, took the 'suggestion' to heart. Except for one.

The recalcitrant office manager didn't like being pressured into making a donation or attending a political fund-raiser. He decided to do something about it. Going to The Washington Post, he told the newspaper what was going on. Electrified by what they heard, The Washington Post ran a big article. This was scandalous stuff. Strong-arming employees for political contributions was against the law. Mandating employee attendance at political functions was tantamount to blackmail.

Of course, the article caught the attention of the Federal Elections Commission (FEC). The FEC investigated the allegations. Contacting Sanford, the FEC asked him if he was aware of the shameful and, if true, highly illegal pressure tactics being used.

Sanford denied any knowledge of the matter. He had placed his trusty lieutenant, one of his best men, in charge of the dinner. The lieutenant's name was James R. Elliot. If the FEC had any further questions, suggested Sanford, they should speak with Elliot.

Following up on Sanford's suggestion, the FEC began an investigation of Elliot. The FEC did not appreciate what they discovered. Elliot had pressured his office managers to make donations and to attend the dinner. Not only that, but Elliot was a convicted felon, who represented the banking industry as an independent sales organization. Elliot's company provided merchant accounts and payment processing equipment for a number of banks. According to the FEC, the situation was unacceptable.

Everybody ran for cover. Except for Elliot. The whole mess was dropped on his front porch.

The FEC fined Elliot and his company, Cherry Communications, Inc., $150,000 for using corporate resources to pressure employees to attend the GOP dinner.[2]

Sanford's bank, First Interstate Bank, and all the other banks did their best imitation of Pontius Pilate. They washed their hands of any complicity. Elliot was tossed into the dumpster with the trash. His services were no longer required or desired.

Elliot did the only thing he knew how to do. He went back to work. Cherry Communications, now limited to pay phones and long-distance telephone service, remained in business. However, Elliot, ever the cowboy, continued to encounter problems. One of his competitors in the pay phone business was a quasi-mystical organization based on somewhat freemasonic fraternal bonds. This organization felt Elliot had stepped across an invisible line, thus violating certain territorial rights and privileges, which the group regarded as exclusive. The group guarded these rights and privileges jealously and with zeal. Elliot was told to back off.

At the time Elliot received this advice, he was building an opulent house in one of Chicago's ritziest neighborhoods. Elliot poured millions of dollars into the construction of the mansion. One night, the mansion

2 'Federal Election Commission Fines,' *PR Newswire*, June 16, 2004.

burned down. Because the surrounding circumstances were mysterious, foul play was a possibility. Perhaps arson. Nothing was ever proven. Accident was the official consensus.

Elliot got the message. He backed off.

Then in 1996, Cherry Communications, accused of illegally switching the long-distance service of more than 7,000 people in California, received a two year suspension from the Public Utilities Commission.[3] In other words, Cherry Communications was prohibited from doing business in California for two years.

Elliot's company was guilty of 'slamming.' Slamming involved switching customers from one long-distance company to another without authorization. More often than not, it was done without the customers' knowledge. It seemed Cherry's agents misrepresented themselves as employees of Pacific Bell and/or forged customer signatures authorizing the change in long-distance service. Most of Cherry's agents employing the devious tactics worked on commission. Some of the agents were convicted felons. When customers complained and didn't pay their bills, Cherry Communications sued them, filing the lawsuits in Chicago.

Elliot refused to comment on the situation. However, company President Dave Giangreco stated that the company had some marketing problems, which were nothing more than growing pains.

"All the problems we encountered are pretty much a microcosm of the failings of the industry," said Giangreco. "It came to our attention late last year that in the course of our sales activity, a small percentage of field representatives have engaged in conduct improper in nature, and the situation was aggravated by a lack of controls."[4]

It was doubtful James R. Elliot was a criminal in the strict sense of the word. What seemed a welter of illegal

---

3 'PUC Slams Door on Carrier for Illegal Switching,' *L.A. Times*, September 7, 1996.

4 Ibid.

activities resolved into clarity and method, once the circumstances were examined. Like a cowboy born 200 years too late, Elliot was out of place. He needed room to roam, to operate. In short, he was an entrepreneur in the broadest and finest sense of the word.

The last time anyone checked, James Elliot was leasing Lear Jets.

Chapter 3
Charlatan

The Merchants Club

California was a beautiful place to live and work during the 1980's. The state was famous for beaches, blondes and babes. And banks. During the late 1980's, a lot of the smaller banks, called savings and loans, were in crisis. They had too much debt and not enough liquidity. It wasn't bad luck or a confluence of circumstances either. The S & Ls had done it to themselves. They got greedy and made bad loans.

Malibu Savings Bank, located in glamorous Malibu, California, had a problem. The bank had pursued an aggressive loan policy for a number of years. Like headhunters, they went looking for people and small businesses that might need a loan. In fact, Malibu Savings Bank was so eager to loan out money that they sometimes forgot to perform credit checks. 'Sometimes' quickly became most of the time. Which meant that most of Malibu's loans were toxic. Malibu Savings Bank had financial cancer.

The prognosis was not good. If something weren't done within the next 90 days, Malibu Savings Bank would bleed to death. The bank needed a transfusion of cash if it wanted to remain in business.

Charles 'Chuck' Burtzloff was one of the officers at Malibu Savings Bank. Smart and ambitious, Burtzloff had a knack for thinking outside the box. When it came to money, he was a creative guy. Restructuring was Burtzloff's specialty. If there were a problem, he would build an answer around the problem, effectively removing it. Occasionally, the construction process was a little left of right.

Confronted with a lack of liquidity, Burtzloff began sifting through possible solutions. As he saw it, the present dilemma was so dire that he needed to set aside the commonly held precepts of the banking industry. An aggressive loan policy had gotten the bank in its present fix. So it appeared that an even more aggressive policy would be required to repair the damage.

Fees were the lifeblood of any bank. Banks tacked on service fees for everything imaginable, especially to merchants. Processing fees, check-cashing fees, account maintenance fees, filing fees, and statement fees. One bank had something called 'generation fees.' No one knew what that was. Not even the bank. Merchants expected to pay fees. In fact, most merchants were so used to paying fees they hardly bothered to examine their monthly statements. They just paid. This sheep-like acceptance made the merchants susceptible.

Burtzloff decided to play off this susceptibility. He came up with a brilliant idea, an innovation so unique, yet so simple that it boggled the mind.

He called it the merchants club. It was a bogus fee that appeared on the monthly statement sent to every merchant account at Malibu Savings Bank. Although the term, *merchants club*, implied membership in an association of businesses, along with as yet unspecified benefits and advantages for members, it was nothing more than a fraudulent hoax. There was no merchants club. And there were no benefits. In fact, it was a service fee. For which no service was provided.

Put simply, the merchant's club fee was a cash grab. A method of getting something for nothing. Commercial real estate developers had used the same idea for years. Only they called their cash grabs 'running a fund raiser.' It went like this: a developer was renovating an old building and found himself short of funds. To raise the money necessary to complete the job, the developer would torch the building. Burn it down. Then he would collect full value for the still-to-be-completed project from his insurance company. It was a quick and easy way to grab the cash. The cash grab made it possible to complete the renovations.

Burtzloff's inventive idea, improvisation at its best, saved Malibu Savings Bank. Millions of dollars of free money funneled into the bank. The merchants paid the fee without asking any questions. Oh, one or two made tentative inquiries, but they were placated with incomprehensible PR jargon. "The bank has instituted a new program that will benefit all its merchant members. The program revolves around merchants endorsing one another to other merchants. In that manner, all of our merchant members benefit."

It was a rip-off of brilliant proportions.

In 1988, Burtzloff left banking. He decided to go into the ISO business. That's where the real action was. While working at Malibu Savings Bank, Burtzloff had noted how payment processing had changed. Technology allowed transactions to happen faster. Credit cards were restructuring the flow of money. Burtzloff decided to bet on facilitating the technological advances.

Calling his company Cardservice International, Burtzloff literally started and then ran his business out of his living room.[5] The primary obstacle for any ISO was account approval. Burtzloff believed he could remove or at least circumvent the obstacle. Hard work, honesty and making good on his promises were the answer. Anyway, that was his pitch.

The reality of the situation was a little different.

In effect, Cardservice International operated like a steam shovel, scooping up everything in sight. The name of the company should have been Shovels 'R Us. The company went after the merchants that other ISOs tried to avoid. Internet start-ups, telephone and mail order shops, and companies involved in the adult entertainment industry.

Porn was big business. Most people didn't know it, but the pornography industry had annual sales revenue of $10 billion. And the U.S. adult-film industry, centered in Los Angeles' San Fernando Valley, was an even larger and more efficient moneymaking machine than legitimate mainstream American cinema. However, the porn industry attracted crooks like bees to a flower. The smell of all that

5 *Greensheet*, March 3, 2001.

money sucked in con artists, cheats, swindlers, and flimflammers. Which meant heavy doses of credit card fraud. Which meant any merchant even remotely connected to the industry was automatically considered high-risk.

"If you look, that's where their growth has been," said one industry observer.[6]

Tim Miller, vice-president of operations denied the allegation. Cardservice International's (CSI) phenomenal growth was not fueled by what was called 'steam heat,' i.e. porn.

"It's a very small portion of our business," said Miller. "But we do have some, since we like to take almost everything that comes to us."[7]

Take everything that comes was Burtloff's motto. In other words, it was a simple numbers game. The more merchants CSI signed up, the more money the company made.

"Our costs are very competitive in our niche, and that niche is high risk as well as across-the-board small to midsize merchants," said Burtzloff. "We focus on what we're good at."[8]

What CSI was good at was signing up high-risk merchants. Merchants classified as high-risk had to pay higher fees for payment processing. This translated to greater profits for CSI. To preclude losses to fraud, CSI installed a high-tech security system. Over 50 security officers monitored incoming transactions closely, watching for fraud either on the part of the consumer or the merchants. Computers flagged transactions that deviated from the norm for any particular business. Once a deviation was detected, security officers made a phone call to the merchant, requesting clarification. If fraud was discovered, CSI pursued criminal prosecution.

First Data Corporation, a superpower in electronic commerce and payment services, noticed the success of CSI. Putting out feelers, First Data began making overtures

6 'Card-Server Business Booming in Cyberspace," *L.A. Times*, December 7, 1999.

7 Ibid.

8 *Greensheet*, March 3, 2001.

to CSI. Burtzloff responded favorably, and First Data acquired 50% of CSI. Four years later, in 2001, First Data would purchase the remaining 50% of the company.

Burtzloff's bet paid off big-time. By 1999, CSI serviced more than 170,000 merchants, which was up by 70,000 from the previous year. CSI processed $500 million in Internet transactions, an increase of 1150% from 1998. Added to that was $4 billion in transactions for traditional brick and mortar retailers, and $4.5 billion for mail/catalog merchants.[9]

Then in April of 2000, Burtzloff really hit the jackpot. He hooked up with WorldPay, which was a global, one-stop provider of end-to-end eCommerce services and multi-currency e-payment systems for small and medium-sized businesses. In simple terms, WorldPay made it possible for customers to pay in local currency while the merchant received payment in its local currency. CSI's merchants had just gone international, which gave them the opportunity for greater profits. And CSI got to tack on another service fee.

Burtzloff foresaw even greater numbers. "I don't think anything can stand in front of the Web growth today," he said. "It's a big, long freight train rolling downhill on a greasy track."

The prediction proved to be true. By 2003, CSI reported processing 125 million transactions, totaling $12 billion in credit card volume.[10] To make sure the numbers increased CSI had a dedicated sales training center in Moorpark, California. CSI brought in its agents, introduced them to new products and service offerings, and told the agents what was working and what was not working. Then the agents went out and sold the new products and services to merchants. Each product and service commanded an appropriate fee, of coursc. Just like in banking, service fees were the lifeblood of payment processing.

CSI was charging lots of fees. Which meant they were making tons of money. CSI looked like a model business.

9 'Card-Server Business Booming in Cyberspace,' *L.A. Times*, December 7, 1999.

10 *Greensheet*, March 3, 2001.

They provided services to merchants. A fee was charged for services rendered. That was the way business worked.

Looks can be deceiving.

Unfortunately, it appeared Burtzloff was still up to his old trick of restructuring. On September 30, 2004, in the Southern District of the U.S. District Court, Thomas Zito et al., filed suit against Leasecomm Corporation and Cardservice International.

What it came down to was this: Leasecomm and Cardservice International were pressuring merchants to sign lease agreements. The agents told the merchants the agreements could be canceled, when in fact the leases were non-cancelable. The agents were also forging signatures on the leases, using bogus witness signatures, and failing to fill out the terms of the leases until after the fact. If merchants failed or refused to make payments, extortionate means were used to collect on the leases, including unauthorized withdrawals from merchants' accounts.

Additionally, Internet Tool Boxes were sold to merchants for $49.95. Supposedly, the boxes would allow merchants to accept credit cards on their web pages. The boxes did *not* make such transactions possible. However, the boxes would work as promised if the merchant purchased additional services from Cardservice "at costs of many thousands of dollars." In other words, the Tool Box was part of a "bait and switch" scheme designed to lure merchants into purchasing ineffective and overpriced products, and lock merchants into long-term contracts.[11]

Cardservice also ran business seminars to educate merchants about the latest innovations and advancements. With this knowledge merchants could enhance their profitability. Or so it seemed. In reality, Cardservice used the seminars to pressure merchants into buying Cardservice products and signing non-cancelable contracts.

It was a cash grab. Only this time it was refined. The old Merchant Club fee had been re-structured into very lucrative, long-term, non-cancelable contracts. The

11 *Thomas ZITO et al., v. LEASECOMM CORPORATION et al.* No. 02 Civ.8074 GEL.

merchants would pay through their noses and Cardservice and Leasecomm would pocket the money.

Leasecomm and Cardservice International had conspired to rip-off merchants. In the end, the two companies settled out of court. An undisclosed sum was paid to the plaintiffs. Neither Leasecomm nor Cardservice acknowledged any wrongdoing.

This wasn't the first time Leasecomm had been sued. The company had a history of participating in such shenanigans. In April of 2003, the Federal Trade Commission had filed a complaint against Leasecomm. The complaint accused Leasecomm of engaging in pyramid schemes, multi-level marketing programs, and fraud.

Leasecomm's outlaw attitude and criminal behavior eventually caught up with it. The company ceased doing business in 2005.

Cardservice International continues to provide services to merchants.

Chapter 4
Interchange Fees

While the independent sales organizations plied their sales skills and signed up merchants for electronic payment processing accounts, the card associations, along with their issuing banks, made their money by charging fees. The fees were called interchange fees. And these fees became a cash cow for Visa, MasterCard and the big banks that issue more than 90% of all MasterCard and Visa cards.

Interchange fees were (and still are) the biggest fees no one ever heard of.

This little known and uncelebrated concept was illustrated by Dee Hock, the creator of Visa. At a speaking engagement, Hock stood before his audience, advocating his unique brand of management. A system of management that revolved around the principles of distributed power, diversity, and ingenuity.

"How many of you recognize this?" he asked, holding out his own Visa card.

Every hand in the audience went up.

"Now," said Hock, "how many of you can tell me who owns it, where it's headquartered, how it's governed, or where to buy shares?"

No one stirred. Not one single hand was raised. No one knew. The reason no one knew was because no one had ever really thought about it.

In other words, Hock had just made his point. "The better an organization is, the less obvious it is," said Hock. "In Visa, we tried to create an invisible organization and keep it that way. It's the results, not the structure or management that should be apparent."[12]

12 'The Trillion Dollar Vision of Dee Hock,' *Fast Company*, April 22, 2010.

The results were profit. And the profit came from fees; interchange fees.

Interchange fees started in the 1970s. Bank of America's BankAmericard, which later became Visa, established the four-party system still utilized today. Essentially, interchange provided an electronic network that acted like a tollbooth. The tollbooth processed the transactions between merchants and banks. Each time a transaction was processed a fee was collected.

The rationale behind interchange fees was open to interpretation. According to Ralph Fontana, "Interchange was a ploy to get member banks involved in the credit card industry." Up until then, member banks did not make much money from late fees and interest charges. Most of their customers were creditworthy and paid off their charges in full every month. When the member banks realized they would collect a fee off of every transaction, they became more prone to play along. The member banks began pushing credit cards.

There was another reason too. According to Professor Adam Levin of Georgetown University Law Center, interchange fees were designed as a way for banks to get around usury and Truth-in-Lending Laws. Banks could only charge so much interest on credit cards without being guilty of usury. Which meant limitations; limitations meant less profit. So if they wanted to make more money, the banks had to find another way. That other way was interchange fees. By charging 'swipe fees,' the banks (and the card associations) effectively raised their interest fees without actually doing so.

It was pure genius.

The four-party system worked like this: the cardholder or customer purchased goods or services from the merchant. The merchant then sold the transaction to the merchant's bank, which was called the 'acquirer.' The merchant's bank sold the transaction to the bank, called the 'issuer', that issued the card. The sale between the 'acquirer' and the 'issuer' took place at the card association's interchange system, which charged a transaction fee.

Along the way, the acquiring bank and the issuing bank each took a cut of the transaction. Thus, at each step of the transaction fees were levied. For example, a consumer purchased $100 of snack foods and beverages for a Super Bowl party. Of that $100, the retailer would receive about $97.50. The remaining $2.50 would be divided up. Visa or MasterCard would receive 1.1% of the $2.50, and an additional 12-cent assessment fee. The bank that issued the card would receive .4% of the $2.50. And the merchant's bank, the 'acquirer,' would get about 7 to 10 cents.

Assessment fees were nothing more than a tax. Visa/MC taxed each transaction simply because they could. It was a way to make more money without actually raising the interchange fee. In other words, it was similar to the airlines charging $25 for each bag checked through or carried on.

On the surface, the interchange concept was simple: a fee was charged for a service provided. However, under the surface, the complexity of interchange fees was intimidating.

Initially, interchange fees encompassed three categories of transactions: restaurants, retail stores, and mail order. Now, though, there are literally hundreds of categories. Both Visa and MasterCard have drawn up intricate fee schedules. Fees vary by merchants' industries, the method of card acceptance, type of card, transaction size and special deals. Face-to-face transactions typically carried a lower fee than mail-order transactions, because they were considered less risky. The fee charged for a card swipe was less than the fee for hand keying. Traditional credit cards carried higher fees than debit cards. And if a merchant accepted rewards cards, the fee was different as well.

This intimidating system of variable fees came into existence as more and more card types entered the picture. In the beginning, there were only basic credit cards. Soon though, there were credit cards, debit cards, business cards, and rewards cards. Each card represented a different type of transaction with a different level of risk attached to it. The result was literally hundreds of interchange categories. Each category carried a different fee. Assigning fees based on so many categories was a nightmare of epic proportions – totally confusing. So to try and simplify the process, a 3-tier system was imposed. Instead of applying hundreds of different fees to innumerable transactions, the fees were categorized into one of three tiers: qualified, mid-qualified or non-qualified.

In 3-tier pricing, a merchant's transactions were placed into one of the three tiers. Each tier charged a different percentage rate on each transaction. The rate charged on any particular transaction was based on a criterion established for each tier.

The Qualified rate was the best rate available. When a merchant accepted a regular consumer credit card and the transaction was processed in a manner defined as 'standard,' the lowest rate was charged. And a merchant's 'qualified' rate was based on the way most of the merchant's transactions would occur. If, for example, the majority of a merchant's transactions occurred over the Internet, the Internet category rate would be defined as Qualified. For a traditional merchant doing business in a mall, only transactions swiped through or read by their in-store terminal would be defined as Qualified.

The Mid-qualified rate was, of course, higher than the Qualified rate. Mid-qualified referred to the amount a merchant was charged when they accepted a credit card that was keyed into the terminal rather than swiped. Rewards cards and/or corporate cards were also categorized as Mid-Qualified. The Mid-Qualified rates were 1.5% to 2.5% higher than the Qualified rate. Since rewards cards account for a large percentage of many merchants' transactions, the Mid-qualified rate ends up costing merchants a lot of money.

Non-qualified was the most expensive of the three rates and included any transaction that did not fall in either the Qualified or Mid-Qualified categories. International and/or government credit cards, along with certain corporate and rewards cards were Non-qualified transactions. Essentially, any transaction that did not use the Address Verification System (AVS), where the billing address did not match the address of the customer's card was penalized by being assigned as Non-qualified. And merchants who did not send their card transactions, known as 'batching', to their banks for payment in a timely manner were given Non-qualified status. Non-qualified rates were 2.00% to 2.5% higher than the Qualified rate, which meant merchants could find themselves paying 4% to 5% on each transaction.

The basic distinction was whether or not the transaction was electronically authorized and captured. In other words, the transaction was either card-present or card-not-present. Card-present transactions took place face-to-face, the merchant could look at the card, which was then swiped through the in-store terminal. Card-not-present transactions occurred when cardholders gave their card number and other information via phone, Internet, fax or mail. Such card-not-present transactions were considered more likely to be fraudulent and therefore more risky. Thus, the transaction was determined to be Non-qualified and a higher rate was charged.

While the 3-tier system sounded simple enough, in reality it was not. For there were tiers within tiers. Both Visa and MasterCard had a number of card-not-present rates. Visa's card-not-present rates distinguished between non-commerce transactions by telephone or mail order; e-commerce transactions that were not authenticated via Verified by Visa; and e-commerce transactions, which the merchant authenticates via Verified by Visa. It goes without saying that each type of transaction was charged a different rate.

In effect, the tier system, which was supposed to simplify the Gordian Knot of fees that merchants paid, did the exact opposite. It geometrically multiplied the rate structure to the point of incomprehensibility. No one except the card associations—Visa, MasterCard, et al.—understood how the system worked, certainly not the merchants.

What was interesting about the 3-tier system was that Visa had no Mid-Qualified or Non-qualified tiers. Visa only had Qualified, which received the lowest rate and everything else, which received the highest rate. Visa didn't need anything else. They had a multiplex of bewildering fee categories at their command. It was the credit card processors that came up with the other two tiers. Why? It was simple. More tiers meant more ways to make money. Any card that did not meet the definition of a 'regular consumer credit card,' such as rewards cards, would automatically be downgraded to a lower tier. A lower tier meant the merchant paid a higher fee.

For example, in restaurants, every transaction fee was based on the most expensive item in a specific category. In other words, the transaction fee collected for the cheapest hamburger on the menu was the same as the most expensive hamburger on the menu. Compounding the problem was the fact that most merchants didn't know what category they fell in. The schedule of fees was so complicated it was impossible to determine. And the statements pumped out by the merchants' ISOs were indecipherable, deliberately so. Supposedly, according to many ISOs, the reason the statements were so abstruse was to thwart the competition. The ISOs didn't want any competing ISO coming in and stealing away a merchant account.

But such explanations were specious at best, outright lies at worst. This obsession for complication was an end in itself. If merchants didn't know how much they were being charged and for what, then they couldn't very well argue their case. It was just like Dee Hock said, "The results were apparent, not the structure." The merchants couldn't understand the structure, yet the results were apparent when the merchants paid fees. Meanwhile, the banks and Visa/MC made money.

An industry insider, Mister X[13], summarized interchange fees in terms most people can understand, but that they don't want to hear. "Interchange is the prime lending rate on credit cards." And he then went on to point out the biggest problem with interchange fees. "The fees never go down. They always go up."

Most merchants agreed with Mr. X. Merchants maintained interchange fees represented "price fixing" by the card associations, which were nothing more than

13 Mr. X is an industry insider who agreed to speak with the authors if, and only if, his anonymity was guaranteed.

"cartels." According to merchants, this price fixing led to three major abuses. First, the interchange fees for U.S. merchants were higher than in other parts of the world, notably Europe. Second, the fees kept going up even as the associated costs - card processing, borrowing, fraud and chargeback costs - had gone down. Third, the fees were non-negotiable. This latter problem was exacerbated by the fact that there were fewer and fewer card issuing banks. The biggest banks accounted for 93% of all cards issued. Which meant they had a monopoly.

Top Five Bank Credit Card Issuers:

Bank Name	Active Accounts
J.P. Morgan Chase	43,000,000
Citigroup	48,000,000
MBNA America	21,000,000
Bank of America	19,000,000
Capital One	24,000,000

Unsurprisingly, the card associations—Visa, MasterCard, American Express, and Discover—and the issuing banks argued otherwise. They asserted that interchange fees were necessary to balance the relative demands of cardholders and merchants. This balance optimized value. In other words, cooperative establishment of fee schedules was not collusion. Rather it was the most efficient and economical means of negotiating between issuing and acquiring banks. The slow but steady rise in fees was reasonable, argued the card associations, especially since more and more customers used cards. This increased usage only served to increase merchant sales and profits. Additionally, the card associations had, through constant vigilance and innovative security systems, reduced credit card fraud.

The crux of the issue, according to the economists, was the system. Card networks were two-sided markets. This meant the card associations catered to two interdependent groups: cardholders and merchants. The card associations (and the issuing banks) had to not only attract cardholders, but also had to induce merchants to accept the cards.

Economists likened the system to that of an auction house. An auction house catered to those wishing to sell and those seeking to buy. Success came from facilitating the needs of both parties. If the auction house expanded, offering more items from more sellers to more seekers, both parties benefited. Likewise, in the context of credit and debit cards, both merchants and customers benefited if the card network expanded.

According to the economists, in such a two-sided market pricing practices that appeared to be monopolistic were, perhaps, not indicative of a monopoly. In other words, interchange fees were not based on cost considerations alone. There was another factor; the "social factor." Customers desired the convenience and ease of credit/debit cards. Matching this desire with the profit-needs of merchants affected the social welfare of both parties. Balancing the social welfare was the burden of card associations.

Although the arguments set forth by the economists sounded good, even the economists admitted they still didn't fully understand two-sided markets. Adequate research had not been done on the subject.

The real question was this: what's going on here?

Two pertinent issues were being overlooked. First, according to industry insiders, the card associations did not negotiate the fees with the issuing banks. The card associations set the fees as high as they could to optimize profits. Each time the fees went up, the card association and the issuing banks made more money. And as long as the issuing banks' profit margins increased they wouldn't complain. Second, and most importantly, while the Federal Reserve Bank regulated the banks that issued credit/debit cards, it did not regulate the credit card industry (the card associations) or its interchangc fees.

Essentially, the card associations did whatever they wanted to do. And what they wanted to do was make a profit. So interchange fees "always went up, never down." At the same time, assessment fees were tacked on, and the fee-based categorical structure became more and more complicated. This strategy made it more difficult to determine if the new rates were actually going up or down. In short, it was a way to maximize income.

Wal-Mart

In the 1990's, Visa promoted a debit card that let consumers access their checking account via the same network that processed Visa's credit cards. The system required a signature from the customer. When the customer used the Visa debit card, it was the equivalent of a cash transaction. Which meant virtually no risk to the merchant or the card association (Visa). Visa set the interchange fee for these 'cash' transactions at 1.35%, and tacked on a 20-cent fee per transaction.

Visa knew easy money when they saw it. So they persuaded the banks to issue more Visa debit cards. Persuading the banks was easy. Visa shared the easy profits with the banks.

What was interesting was that for the same service, the other networks charged less than a dime. Of course, those networks did not require a signature, operating on a 4-digit PIN instead.

Visa defended signature debit by saying the fee was justified because it (signature debit) was more convenient than PIN debit. The convenience argument was based on the fact that at the time only about 15% of merchants had keypads for entering a PIN. In that sense, then, the argument held up. Most merchants had the capability to accept signature debit cards. Thus, signature debit cards were more 'convenient.' But the fee Visa charged for convenience was stiff. Indeed, it was more than stiff, it was outrageous. Visa was exploiting the situation. It was sheer profiteering.

As usual, there was more to it. Visa had an "honor all cards" rule. If a merchant chose to accept Visa's credit cards, the merchant was required to honor Visa's debit cards. In other words, the merchant had no choice but to continue taking the debit cards, despite the higher fees. It was Visa's game and the game was played by Visa's rules. All the merchants could do was ante up.

Many merchants thought the cards were stacked. There was no way to win.

Wal-Mart, Sears, Circuit City, and Safeway decided they didn't like the way the game was played. They were tired of anteing up millions of dollars in fees every year. So they sued. In court, their attorneys argued that Visa's requirement to "honor all cards" was improper. Fees for various types of cards should be set in proportion to the risk each transaction posed to the network. Since Visa's debit cards were tantamount to cash, there was very little risk. Therefore, the fees should be adjusted accordingly.

Visa's attorneys argued otherwise, citing convenience and the delicate balance between customers and merchants. The litigation went on for seven years, as each side filed motions and counter-motions. In the end (2003), Visa and MasterCard agreed to end the "honor all cards" rule as related to debit cards. The card associations also agreed to temporarily reduce debit card fees and establish lower transaction fees. And Visa and MasterCard agreed to pay the retailers a settlement of $3 billion over ten years. Visa paid $2 billion and MasterCard paid $1 billion.

However, the settlement did not address requirements for merchants to accept premium credit cards. Which meant merchants remained obligated to take premium credit cards at the established interchange fees. And those fees, since they were not addressed, could go up at any time.

According to Visa and MasterCard, the lawsuit was "much ado about nothing."[14] To support this statement, Visa offered data showing that only a handful of retailers stopped accepting Visa debit cards.

A Funny Thing Happened

A lot of merchants believed that, as a result of the lawsuit, interchange fees would start to decrease across the board. This decrease would reflect a new spirit of competition between the card associations. Since competition was the lifeblood of the free market system, the merchants felt the monopolistic stranglehold of the card associations was finally over.

14 'How Visa, Using Card Fees, Dominates a Market,' *The New York Times*, January 5, 2010.

The merchants who believed this were dreaming. A funny thing happened. Although Visa temporarily reduced its fees for signature debit cards, as per the terms of the settlement, Visa raised the fees on PIN debit transactions. The smart guys at Visa figured if they couldn't make money one way, they'd simply do it another way. Visa ran an end-around play. The fee for PIN debit transactions went from 20 cents to 90 cents.

Lo and behold, the member banks began pushing PIN debit cards to consumers, which meant the merchants had to accept them if they wanted to do business.

The other card association, MasterCard, followed Visa's lead. It also raised the fees on PIN debit cards.

When the merchants screamed 'foul,' Visa had a glib explanation. Visa denied any kind of 'push' by its member banks. Visa said its PIN debit network took off, despite the rising fees, because it gave merchants, banks, and consumers a level of efficiency and security that was unmatched. In other words, it was the same old song and dance. As Visa put it, "We are motivated as a company to try to drive value to each one of those participants (merchants, banks and consumers) so that they accept the card, issue more cards, use the card."[15]

Of course, Visa encouraged more merchants, banks and consumers to use their cards. Every time a card with the Visa logo on it was swiped anywhere in the world, the money machine went ka-ching. Visa made money. The banks made money. The merchants and the consumers paid the fees. The "drive to value" accrued only to the banks and the card association.

In the real world, interchange fees have proven to be a very blunt instrument. At the Ula Café, which is a neighborhood coffeehouse in Jamaica Plain, Massachusetts, there's a sign posted on the cash register. The sign informs customers that every time they pay with plastic money, it costs the coffee shop 25 cents. For that reason, the coffees shop encourages customers to pay cash for purchases less than $10.

The owner of Ula Café tried to negotiate a reduction in fees with her bank. The bank told her there was no way.

15 Ibid.

Based on the type of business, purchase amounts, payment product type, and processing technology the café used, the fees were non-negotiable. So the sign went up on the cash register and the Ula Café no longer accepts American Express cards, no matter what the amount of the purchase.[16] Only Visa, MasterCard and Discover are accepted and even then only for purchases greater than $10.[17]

Over in Boston, an events company called The Second Glass tacks a surcharge on ticket sales, even though Visa and MasterCard expressly forbid surcharges. The reason surcharges are forbidden is simple. Visa and MasterCard do not collect a percentage of surcharges. The surcharges go to the merchant. Which means Visa and MasterCard are being cut out of more profit. Companies that violate the surcharge rule face stiff penalties, including fines and the loss of their ability to accept Visa and MasterCard cards.

Tyler Balliet, the honcho at Second Glass, says he is aware that his company is violating the card associations' rules. "We just had to do what all the big guys do: we passed our fees on to consumers," says Baillet. "We try to minimize this fee (shipping and handling charges), but if we ate that, we'd have to raise ticket prices anyway."

Either way, whether by surcharge or higher ticket prices, the fees are being passed along to consumers. However, utilizing a surcharge allows Second Glass to keep the amount passed on to the consumer lower than if Second Glass raised the ticket prices. If the ticket prices were raised, Visa and MasterCard would take a percentage. This, in turn, would mean Second Glass would have to raise its prices again to cover the percentage.

16 Generally speaking, American Express fees are about 1% higher than the other card associations. For this reason, some merchants refuse to accept American Express.

17 Up until 2010, merchants refusing to accept credit cards for transactions of any amount were in violation of the card associations' rules. Due to legislation, after 2010, merchants were allowed to refuse credit cards for transactions less than $10.

In other words, it's a vicious cycle. And once the cycle starts, there's no way to stop it. That's what the card associations are counting on.

Chapter 5
Marty the Magnificent

The secretary said, "Mr. Fontana, your next appointment is here."

"Okay," replied Ralph Fontana. "What's his name?"

"Marty."

Fontana nodded. "Send him in. Let's see if he can sell."

Marty didn't come in. Marty entered. Marty performed. Marty waltzed to a chair and sat down.

Fontana liked what he saw. The guy made a good impression. Looked like an older version of Elvis.

Marty wore flash threads, very stylish. "I saw your ad in the newspaper. For sales reps," said Marty, in a dripping accent. The kind of accent that spread slow, thick and gooey like warm Velveeta.

Marty grinned. "Just moved to Vegas from New Orleans, where I ran for mayor." He raised his eyebrows, pitching candor at Fontana. "I lost."

Fontana laughed. "I kind of figured that, since you're here and not down in New Orleans running the show."

Marty showed Fontana his mayoral candidate's smile, winking. "Too bad. I'd have made a great politician. Sales are my thing. I sell voters. I sell policy. I sell myself."

"How about merchants?" asked Fontana. "Can you sell to merchants? We set up their credit card processing agreements and you can make a lot of money because of the leases involved."

"It would behoove ya' to hire me," drawled Marty, with a twinkle in his eyes. "The merchants and Fairway West will wonder how they ever got along without me." 'It would behoove ya" was Marty's favorite expression, matching or exceeding Algonquin J. Calhoun in it's delivery. Yes, Marty was indeed from New Orleans.

Fairway West was a nationwide credit card ISO. The western region of Fairway headquartered in Las Vegas, and Ralph Fontana was the honcho.

Fontana liked this guy more and more. He was smooth. Maybe too smooth. But the best reps were smooth and confident. And this guy had copious amounts of both qualities.

"When do I start?" asked Marty, flashing his headliner smile.

Fontana laughed. "Tomorrow."

It turned out Marty was right. He *was* a great salesman.

Marty went to work; Marty didn't just sell—Marty did business. Marty trafficked. Marty persuaded, cajoled and convinced. Marty finalized. Merchants signed on one after another.

Marty wasn't simply a great salesman; *he was awesome!* In fact, he was so awesome that Fontana got a little suspicious. When reps exceeded even the highest expectations, it was usually for one of two reasons. Either the rep was working his butt off, putting in 18-hour days, seven days a week. Or the guy was plain cheating in some way. Marty was a hard worker, but he wasn't killing himself off. Fontana wondered if Marty might be doctoring his paperwork.

So Fontana checked Marty out. He scrutinized Marty's paperwork. There was nothing wrong with it. It was all straightforward. The t's were crossed; the i's were dotted. No hanky panky. Fontana made some phone calls. He called the merchants, asked if they'd signed on with Fairway West. The merchants said yes. Who was the sales rep? Marty, said the merchants. Fontana shrugged. He couldn't find anything amiss. Marty was just one heck of a sales rep.

After work, Marty hung out at the hot nightspots downtown that newbies to Las Vegas were prone to go to, places like the Golden Nugget. He had a few drinks, made a few friends, and passed out his cards to pretty girls. Marty liked pretty girls. At 44 years of age, Marty was in his prime. He had a 19-year old fiancé named Melissa, who would be following him out to Vegas soon. Right now,

Melissa was back in New Orleans. As soon as Marty was settled in, she'd make a beeline for Sin City.

Marty deployed his business cards like a fisherman making a cast. The cards were bait. It worked like this: Marty would see some young, pretty girl sitting at the bar, nursing a drink. More often than not, the pretty girl had just arrived in Vegas from some Midwestern Podunk town, where the most exciting summer activities were dodging tornadoes and going to the movies. In the winter, they shoveled snow and went to the movies. Bored out of their gourds, the pretty girls decided to get out of town and get a life. They flocked to Vegas, where in descending order they hoped to make it as showgirls, card dealers, or cocktail waitresses. In short, they wanted to work in the casinos.

For pretty girls, getting a job in Vegas was hard. There were lots of pretty girls. And they were all applying for the same jobs. It wasn't what you knew or how pretty you were; it was *whom* you knew. Marty knew this. So Marty carried around a stack of business cards. He had cards from almost every casino exec in town. Acquiring the cards was simple in Marty's World. He waltzed into the casinos like Rumpelstiltskin and proceeded to spin a golden tale. He was bringing his entire entourage from New Orleans, where he was running for Mayor, to Vegas, where the victory party would be held. That's why Marty was there. He was reconnoitering for likely landing spots, places with *beau coup* action. Marty had high roller written all over him. Everyone from the CEO of the casino to the blackjack pit boss smelled the sweet incense of money. They kowtowed as they gave him their cards and several more for his influential friends. Marty had hundreds of cards saved, and used them like the professional he was.

His collection of cards allowed Marty to be anyone he wanted to be in the casino industry. One night he might be a vice-president of operations or director of entertainment for the MGM Grand or Caesar's Palace. The next night he would be the show director for the Stardust. In other words, Marty was somebody. Marty was connected.

Armed with his arsenal of cards, Marty went hunting. Like a big-game hunter on safari in Africa, Marty stalked his prey.

Marty sat down next to a pretty girl and started talking. Marty rapped. Marty conversed. Marty told great jokes. Marty bought drinks. As the evening progressed, Marty moved in, asking questions. Where was she from? What did she do? What did she want to do?

Marty listened. Marty empathized. Marty acted interested. Depending on the resistance, if any, the attractiveness, and the gullibility of the young lady, Marty would decide who he wanted to be that night. He gave the pretty girl his card, MGM Grand, VP of Operations. The girl's eyes went wide. The girl was impressed. Marty was impressed that she was impressed.

"Come around tomorrow or the next day," said Marty. He flicked the card with his finger. "Ask for me at the desk. I'll be your foot in the door. I'll get you a job at the MGM. We're always on the lookout for talented, beautiful women." Marty flashed his pearly whites. "I'm pretty sure I can get you a spot in our big revue. You know, bright lights, sequins, frilly feathers. You won't be the star, but with your looks—hey, it won't be long. And the money, honey, is great."

Marty smoothed the air with his hand. "Easy street and high-rollers." He laughed.

Marty enticed. Marty cajoled. Marty sold. Marty did business.

The pretty girl ended up in a hotel room with Marty, where she demonstrated her gratitude in very palpable terms.

The next afternoon, the pretty girl sashayed into the MGM Grand, asking for Bob Smith or whatever alias Marty was using at the time.

"Hold one," replied the blonde cutie pie at the desk.

More often than not, the pretty girl's name would be relayed via telephone to the executive in question. Even though he didn't recognize her name, he would have her escorted to his office. Casino execs didn't want to insult anyone. She had his card, and casino execs didn't just give their card to *everyone*. And if the pretty girl mentioned their "meeting" the previous evening to the receptionist, she would gain *immediate* entrance. Casino execs didn't want any issues or rumors flying among the staff.

After meeting the person whose name was on the card, the result was invariably the same.

"Somebody took you for a ride," said the blonde receptionist, as she led the pretty girl back out. A look, conveyed in intra-cultural girl-code, passed between the two. Nothing overt was said, yet volumes were spoken.

"I'm sorry," said the blonde.

"Not as sorry as I am."

The pretty girl turned and walked out of the MGM Grand.

Marty continued to use his unique and proven social networking scam as long as he was in Vegas – even after his fiancée, Melissa, came to town. He never got caught.

One day, Ralph Fontana got a call. It was Marty. He was in jail and needed someone to come down and bail him out. Fontana drove down to LVPD and bailed Marty out. In the car, on the way back, Marty explained.

"Before I came out here from New Orleans, I bought a car. I gave the guy a check. Because of some clerical mistake, a misunderstanding at the bank, the check didn't clear," said Marty.

"It bounced," said Fontana.

Marty rolled his eyes. "Yeah. Anyway, I was unaware that the check hadn't cleared. The guy reported the car stolen, which wasn't the case of course. A simple mistake that spiraled out of control. So last night, I came out of the bar and imagine—they're towing my car."

Fontana laughed. He knew what was coming next. "And you said something, right?"

"For sure," asserted Marty. "I had no idea they were operating under a misperception. So naturally, I said, 'What in the hell do you think you're doing? Towing my car?'"

Fontana roared with laughter.

Marty beamed his smile. "They arrested me. Can you beat that? Over some itty-bitty check that didn't clear."

Fontana just laughed and drove Marty home.

Fairway West had a big account with one of the casinos in Laughlin, Nevada—eighteen terminals. The account was large enough to warrant special attention. Ralph Fontana wanted to make sure any little glitches were remedied immediately. He didn't want little problems mutating into monstrous-sized problems. Little problems could be handled right away. If they weren't, they grew and grew and grew. Pretty soon Godzilla was running amuck. Which meant mobilizing the National Guard.

Johnny-on-the-spot customer service was what was needed, Fontana decided. Fairway would put a PR-rep in Laughlin. That way, potential problems would go away rather than metastasize.

Fontana rummaged through his personnel, deciding whom to send. By definition, a PR rep had to excel in social skills, being gregarious and intelligent. A PR rep had to be smooth. Yet he/she had to know the system well enough to solve problems and fix them. As he thought about it, Fontana decided that really there was only one person, outside of himself, for the job.

Fontana still considered Marty someone who could dance on his feet and handle any situation. It wasn't until later, after Marty had vamoosed, that Fontana began finding out about all Marty's peccadilloes, such as handing out sham business cards to scared, lonely young ladies. Fontana was nobody's fool. He'd been around the block more than once. But Marty was magnificent. Marty fooled everybody. He even tricked Fontana with his smooth-ass lying politician's camouflage.

Fontana mentioned the Laughlin gig to Marty.

Marty loved the idea. PR rep/customer service was right up his alley. All he had to do was schmooze and hang out in the casino. And maybe every once in a while he'd be called upon to take care of some business. Free and easy-does-it. Lots of latitude to develop his attitude.

Marty packed his bags, which was the most difficult part of the whole job. And even though Fontana had leased a company apartment for him in Laughlin and paid his other expenses, Marty knew he would need some cash-for-flash in his pockets. He had around 40 custom suits he'd bought at Dillard's in New Orleans. Like Marty's car, the suits were also paid for by check. Somewhere between $40,000 and $100,000 worth of swank threads. Most still had the sales tags on them. He couldn't take them all, so Marty had to cull the herd, perform suit triage. It took a while, but he eventually decided which ones he would return and which ones he would keep.

Marty took the runners-up to the Vegas Dillard's, where he asked for a cash refund. Renowned for their no-questions-asked return policy, Dillard's complied. When Marty walked out of the store, he was ready to travel—light, tight, and flush with cash. He never knew when he might need to show the roll of hundreds to someone.

Once his car was loaded, Marty smoothed his hair back and headed south. The Emerald of the Desert—Las Vegas—receded in his rearview mirror. He was on his way to Laughlin. And he had *a lot* of time to think about his next career move.

Laughlin sat on the extreme southern tip of Nevada. Situated next to the Colorado River, Laughlin sat on one side of the river. On the other side of the river sat Bullhead City, Arizona. The combined population of the two cities was around 50,000 people, with Bullhead accounting for the lion's share.

Laughlin was unique. It wasn't really a city. The Clark County Board of Commissioners governed it. The Commissioners took advice from the Laughlin Town Advisory Board, which was an appointed body headed up by the Town Manager. Even more bizarre was the fact that police services were provided by the Las Vegas Police Department. Las Vegas was 94 miles north of Laughlin, which meant the LVPD covered a lot of ground.

Laughlin got its name from Don Laughlin, who was originally from Minnesota. Laughlin owned the 101 Club in Las Vegas. He bought the southern tip of Nevada in 1964. Back then; the place was called South Pointe. Laughlin's grand plan was to open a casino in South Pointe. He did just that, opening the Riverside Resort, which offered all-you-can-eat dinners for 98-cents, 12 slot machines, two gaming tables, and 8-motel rooms. Don Laughlin wanted to call the town 'Riverside' or maybe 'Casino.' However, he was overruled by the U.S. Post Office, which named the town Laughlin.

Laughlin, Nevada was RV heaven. Recreational vehicles from all over North America trundled in and out of the place year round. In fact, Laughlin was onc of the top 5 most popular destinations for RV enthusiasts. Because of this, Laughlin didn't have the glitz and glamour or the adult entertainment of Las Vegas or Reno. Billing itself as "family-friendly," Laughlin attracted people by emphasizing outdoor and family activities.

Make no mistake, Laughlin had lots of gambling. Gambling was the premiere attraction. For that's where the money was. Even though Laughlin's gamblers arrived in RVs, with their kids in tow, they were still looking for a good time. During the day, they wanted hiking, fishing, biking, and boating. At night, they wanted games of chance, booze, and stage shows.

By the time Marty showed up, the action in Laughlin had grown to equal most of the casinos on The Strip in Vegas. Hundreds of slots, legions of gaming tables and roulette wheels, and hundreds of rooms. They even had their own cattle ranch in order to provide the steaks used in the casino restaurants.

All this action operated on money. People had to pay to play.

To access their money, the RV'ers used plastic. They swiped their plastic credit cards through terminals. If the terminals didn't go, the cash didn't flow.

Marty was in Laughlin to facilitate the flow of cash. His job was to make sure the terminals functioned as smooth as cashmere.

Marty had a lot of time on his hands. Which meant Marty did a lot of thinking. Marty was an opportunist, always looking for new, creative ways to make money with little or no work. Marty chewed over ways to make money fast.

Sitting in unique Laughlin, Marty perceived a unique opportunity. Marty decided to act.

Ralph Fontana's phone rang. It was his secretary. He had a call from First Tennessee. First Tennessee was the processor. They processed the transactions on the 18 terminals at Riverside Resort.

"How can I help you?" inquired Fontana.

"This is Nadine. New accounts at First Tennessee."

"Just a quick question," said Nadine. "On the Riverside Resort checking account. Did you want the new address or the old address?"

Fontana had a premonition. Fontana frowned. "I'm not sure. What new account?"

"Riverside Resort opened a new checking account. But they neglected to indicate if there was a new address or not," explained Nadine.

"I wasn't aware of any new account," said Fontana. "Let me call down there and see what's ticking. I'll find out which address they want to use."

"Certainly," said Nadine. She laughed. "That way we won't make any mistakes. Let me give you my number."

Fontana jotted down the number. "I'll call you right back."

After he hung up, Fontana asked his secretary for the file for Riverside. When there wasn't a copy of the New Account in the folder, he asked her if she knew anything about the account. She didn't.

Acting on intuition, he decided to call Riverside rather than Marty. He asked about the new checking account. There was no new checking account.

Fontana called Nadine at the Bank of Tennessee. Fontana told Nadine he had just spoken with the business office at Riverside Resort. He explained that it was Karma that she had called him since they had decided to cancel the account change anyway, so just go ahead and destroy the change document. But would she please make a copy and fax it to him first, since his office inadvertently failed to make a copy of it. Nadine happily agreed and in a few minutes Fontana had the copy of the account change as well as a voided copy of the check.

There were two reasons for this little subterfuge. Fontana did not want First Tennessee to know how close they all had come to disaster. He ran a crackerjack organization, and aside from a few merchants, who attempted to defraud the bank, it was a smooth, growing, profitable company. If something like this got out, it would change everything. They wouldn't trust any deal he sent forward from that day on.

In addition, as soon as he heard about a 'missing' change of account, he had a funny feeling about what might be going on, especially since Marty was in Laughlin. It was just too coincidental. The whole thing had Marty's *modus operandi* written all over it.

He was right. This was what happened.

Looking at the documents that Nadine had faxed him, Fontana could see that Marty had filled out the 'Change of Account' form, going so far as signing it as the responsible company representative. At the same time, Marty had opened up a Business Checking account, under the name of Riverside Resort Spa, with a bank in Las Vegas. Close to, but not the same as, Riverside Resort. Marty then mailed the Change of Account form to First Tennessee, asking that they put a rush on the change! Which they did!

No one noticed anything was out of order, including anyone at the bank where the account was opened or at First Tennessee. Marty forged the signature on the account change. Marty's big, and fatal, mistake was that he failed to designate a new address or the old address. If he hadn't made this mistake, the bank wouldn't have called. The weekend's revenue at Riverside Resort, approximately $500,000, would have been deposited in the new account on Tuesday. Marty would have walked away with half a million dollars in cash. And no one would have known for a few days. By the time anyone caught on, Marty would have been long gone.

Reaching for his car keys, Ralph Fontana walked out to his Cadillac. Ninety minutes later, he arrived in Laughlin.

Marty was already gone. The apartment was completely empty. Even the furniture was gone. Marty had either sold it or taken it with him.

Fontana said, "He must have figured out that we were on to him. Somehow he intuited it. I never heard from him again. Never talked to anyone who knew anything about him ... I knew from my past experiences with the Las Vegas Police that there was little they could do. I considered myself lucky to have caught it when I did, and before the worst happened."

Back in Las Vegas, Fontana began noticing a lot of chargebacks, which were first payment defaults. Merchants were defaulting on their lease payments.

Generally speaking, chargebacks didn't happen frequently. This sudden rash of chargebacks was highly unusual. Something was wrong. Fontana began investigating. In all, there were 38 chargebacks. And guess what? Marty was the rep on all of them.

After more investigation, it became obvious what had happened. Marty signed up 38 dead people. He got the social security numbers of recently deceased individuals from the country clerk. He wrote them up as merchants, assigning names to the businesses. Marty turned the leases over to Fairway.

Fairway's policy was to call each merchant to confirm the lease. Once confirmation was received, the rep was paid his commission on the lease.

Marty knew the system. Marty beat the system. Besides casinos, Las Vegas had lots of telemarketing companies. Marty had a lady friend at one of the big telemarketers.

Marty enticed. Marty greased the wheels. Marty paid his friend to participate in the scam.

Marty put the telemarketer's number down on the non-existent merchants' leases, along with a notation of the best time to call. Fairway West would call to confirm the lease. Marty's friend, pretending to be the merchant, would say, "Yes, we signed the lease." Confirmation. Marty was paid his commission.

Ralph Fontana figured Marty made $40,000 to $50,000 on the 38 leases. Smooth operator.

While telling the Marty story, a fond smile tweaked the corners of Ralph Fontana's mouth.

"I've tried to find out where Marty is," said Fontana. "I'd like to take him out for a drink. If nothing else, just to find out what he has done for the last twenty years or so. And the strange thing is that I am not mad at the guy; it was hard to get mad at Marty. I have some relatives and friends in law enforcement and they tell me it's the same feeling that they have for a thief who is a real professional. Marty was, without a doubt, the most charming guy I have ever met. The guy was a one-of-a-kind character, one I'll never forget. Talk about smooth. Marty was like silk."

Fontana laughed. "I can't prove it, but it is my opinion that Marty's scam was the reason the rules changed. After Marty, sales reps not only had to provide telephone numbers for new merchants, but also photographs of the place of business."

Ralph Fontana was in Atlanta, heading up Universal Savings Bank in the southeastern part of the country. A national credit card processing company, USB was growing by leaps and bounds. Business was good.

USB had plush offices in a modern business park. The offices had space to move around in and views. A guy came in looking for a job—sales rep. He looked like Fat Albert, the character made famous by Bill Cosby.

Fontana needed sales reps. Fat Albert was hired.

Right off the bat, Fat Albert started making sales. Too many. Fontana was older and wiser to the ways and shenanigans of sales reps. He double-checked all Fat Albert's leases. He couldn't find anything wrong with them.

One day, Fat Albert strolled into Fontana's executive office, which had executive views.

"I'm moving to Nashville," announced Fat Albert.

"We'll be sorry to lose you," said Fontana. USB didn't have a branch in Nashville.

Fat Albert cracked his knuckles. "What would you think about opening up an office in Nashville?" asked Fat Al. "I could run it for you." He glanced at Fontana to see if he was impressed.

Fontana considered the idea for a moment. "I like it. It's probably time to push the envelope a little bit. Nashville's a big city. Expanding into the area makes sense."

Fat Al smiled. "Excellent. I'll be up there looking for a place to live. I'll check it out, see what kind of office space is available."

Fontana nodded. "Sounds good. Let me know what you find. I'll get things moving on this end."

Fat Albert left. That was the last Ralph Fontana heard of him. It was as if Fat Albert dropped off the face of the earth.

One day Ralph Fontana got a call from an Atlanta merchant.

"I'm wondering when I'm going to get my Gold American Express business card?" said the merchant.

"Your what?" asked Fontana.

"My Gold American Express business card," repeated the merchant. "Your sales representative told me I'd get a Gold AmEx card as a perk for signing up with ya'll."

Fontana smiled, shaking his head. What was this merchant talking about? "I'm sorry, but we don't provide credit cards for merchants. We process transactions. We don't issue credit cards."

"Well, that's not what your salesman said. He said that your bank had a special relationship with American Express, and your bank was the only processor in the country that had this offer." The merchant was getting hot under the collar. He thought Fontana was brushing him off.

"What was the salesman's name?" asked Fontana.

"Albert. A big, heavyset guy," asserted the merchant.

After investigating further, Ralph Fontana discovered why Fat Albert was such a great sales rep. Fat Al was enticing merchants to sign leases by telling them they would receive Gold American Express business cards. The gold cards carried high credit limits.

Fat Albert was running a scam. Every new merchant needed access to credit, and Fat Albert had the perfect sales pitch. Because of the promised gold card, the merchants signed. Fat Al told the merchants their cards would arrive in six to eight weeks. Fat Albert collected his commissions from legitimate leases. Only the conditions of the leases were misrepresented. There were no gold cards.

After waiting six to eight weeks, the merchants started calling the office. "Where's my gold card? Your rep promised me a gold card."

Fat Albert was already gone. He had timed it just right. Make a busload of sales by promising gold cards, and then just as the cards should be arriving, move to Nashville. Or where ever it was he really went.

Chapter 6
Beer Money (Fees)

The card associations—Visa, MasterCard, Discover, and American Express—make a great deal of money on fees. Swipe fees alone accounted for $46 billion in 2009. Then there are Dues and Assessments, which, no matter what they're called, are nothing more than additional fees. Dues and Assessments are established by Visa and MasterCard, and are the same for every processor in the industry. These fees, Dues and Assessments, are paid by the Acquiring Banks (merchants' banks) directly to Visa and MasterCard.

And don't forget the Authorization fee, which is the fee every credit card processing company pays to route transactions through the credit card processing networks. Processing networks house vast servers that are responsible for authorizing credit cards in real-time, transmitting data back and forth between banks and merchants. Authorization fees vary, ranging between 8 cents and 15 cents per transaction. And the fee applies whether the request is approved or not.

The Authorization fee should not be confused with the Transaction fee or the Per Item fee, which are separate and extra fees.

Essentially, the credit card industry runs on fees. Fees are the driving force, the guts, of the industry. Without fees, profits would plunge. And not just for the card associations and their co-conspirators, the banks, but also for the ISOs and Merchant Account Providers (MAP).

When a sales rep walks into a merchant's place of business, the first thing the merchant asks is, "What's your rate?" The question refers to the interchange percentage fee. And most reps, since they aren't stupid and want the merchant's business, quote the lowest rate possible, which is the Qualified rate. Only most reps, because they want to stay in business, which means they need to make a profit, usually quote the Qualified rate plus a little mark-up. This little mark-up is what used to keep the ISOs and the MAPs in business.

But not anymore.

Nowadays, merchants want the lowest possible rate. So the mark-ups have gotten smaller and smaller. To the point of being almost non-existent. The ISOs can't make enough profit off the mark-ups to remain in business. Which means they, the ISOs and MAPS, depend on fees to make a living.

As Ralph Fontana explained, "Merchants want a low rate, so processors make money off fixed fees. It's become a fixed fee business."

This translates into a number of add-on fees, some of which are legitimate and some of which are not. So-called legitimate fees include:

BILL BACK FEES: Bill back fees occur when the merchant receives his monthly statement. The statement shows that the merchant has paid the interchange percentage rate on transactions that have already occurred. This is as it should be. Transactions took place and the interchange fee was deducted. What's not as it should be is that the merchant then pays all the other fees—transaction fees, per item fees, authorization fees, etc. —on the next month's statement. In other words, the other fees are not charged during the month in which they occurred. Instead, the fees for one month are paid on the next month's statement. They are "billed back."

The result is total confusion on the part of the merchant. The amount of time it takes to research the actual cost per transaction is tremendous, if it can be done at all. In the end, the merchant never really knows precisely how much he's paying for the privilege of accepting credit cards.

STATEMENT FEES: Every month merchants receive an account statement from their providers. The statement shows how much credit/debit card activity the merchant did during the month and what fees the merchant was charged. More often than not, statement fees are not directly related to the cost of generating "paper" statements. Rather, they are related to the general overhead costs of the provider. Which means the statement fee would not be waived if the merchant elected to receive "paperless" statements.

Simply put, providers charge merchants a separate and additional fee for telling the merchant how much he is being charged in fees. The merchant is paying for a service that won't even tell him what services he is paying for unless he pays another fee.

The statement fee is the ultimate Catch-22. The merchant cannot be told what he is being charged without paying another charge to learn what he is being charged.

Monthly minimum fee: This fee is 'industry standard,' which means it is universally applied to all merchant accounts. Every merchant pays a monthly minimum fee. Merchants pay this fee to their providers for keeping their account active. If the merchant's credit/debit card processing activity does not equal or exceed the monthly minimum, the merchant is charged the minimum amount, regardless. This fee is a way for providers to ensure profitability.

For example, Bob's Java Shoppe has signed a contract with a $50 monthly minimum fee. If in June, due to scorching weather, no one wants to buy hot coffee, Bob's Java Shoppe doesn't do much business. In fact, all Bob's customers desire bottled water or iced tea, and pay for it with cash. The result is that Bob's Java Shoppe only generates $15 in credit/debit card processing fees for the month of June. Nevertheless, Bob's Java Shoppe will be charged the $50 monthly minimum fee. And note that the statement fee discussed above, along with all the other 'standard' fees, are not part of the monthly minimum fee. All the other fees and the monthly minimum fee have to be paid, if the merchant wants to continue to accept credit/debit cards.

In today's world, any merchant who decided not to accept credit/debit cards would rapidly join the dinosaurs in the land of extinction. This stark reality means that the card associations are sitting in the catbird seat. If merchants want to stay in business and be competitive, they must provide service. Part of service is convenience.

And convenience means accepting credit/debit cards. Merchants have no option. They pay.

Batch fees: The batch fee is charged to merchants every time the merchants 'settle' their terminals. Settling a terminal—also referred to as 'batching'—occurs when merchants send their daily transactions to their acquiring bank for payment. Some providers perform this service automatically for their merchants. It is vital that merchants settle their terminals on a daily basis. If they do not, the card associations impose higher fees as a penalty.

What the batch fee boils down to is this. If a merchant wants to receive payment for goods or services he has sold, he has to pay a fee. For example, it is the middle of January and Bob's Java Shoppe is doing a brisk business. It is snowing outside and bitterly cold. The baristas hustle all day long to fill the orders of a never-ending line of shivering customers. At the end of the long day, Bob settles his terminal. He wants to be paid so he can continue to pay his baristas. Once the terminal is settled, the card associations immediately get their share, as do the banks and the processors. But not Bob. Before Bob gets his share of his money, he has to pay a batch fee.

In effect, Visa and MasterCard are charging Bob a fee for paying them a percentage of his money.

Customer service fee: This fee is charged by some providers to pay for the cost of customer service. It is a legitimate and necessary fee. If a terminal malfunctions or the merchant has a question, customer service reps have to be available to handle the problem.

Chargeback fee: Chargebacks are not the same as refunds, which is simply a merchant refunding a transaction. Chargebacks occur when the cardholder disputes a transaction with a merchant. When this happens, a chargeback fee is assessed whether the chargeback is successful or not. The cardholder's bank presents the chargeback to the merchant's credit card processing bank. Usually, such complaints revolve around the fact that the cardholder does not remember the transaction. More often than not, the potential chargeback is resolved when the merchant's bank provides details about the disputed transaction. This service is called a 'retrieval request.' And some providers charge an additional fee for it.

Occasionally, chargebacks occur because of fraud. However, no matter what the reason, a chargeback results in a chargeback fee to the merchant. Typically, the chargeback fee is $15 to $30, plus the transaction fee and the amount processed. Under Visa and MasterCard's rules, the merchant's processing bank is responsible for all the merchant's transactions. Both Visa and MasterCard require that any merchant's chargebacks account for 1% or less of the merchant's total dollar volume. If the percentage of chargebacks exceeds 1%, the merchant's bank is fined. Fines start at $5000 to $25,000. And of course, the fine is passed on to the merchant.

According to Ralph Fontana, the following fees are cash grabs. "These cash grab fees are put in place to keep profit margins where they should be."

Annual fee: This fee is charged by providers to pay for the cost of maintaining the merchant's account. Such fees may be charged annually or quarterly, depending upon the provider. Annual fees range from $79 to $399.

The Annual fee is bogus. It is redundant, as the merchant is already paying a monthly minimum fee to maintain his account.

Peak season fee: This fee is charged by providers for processing an above-normal number of transactions during 'busy seasons.' The thinking behind the Peak season fee is that an extraordinary number of transactions require an additional fee. For example, Christmas would be classified as a Peak season, because of increased transactions, which have to be processed. Therefore, merchants are charged an additional fee, which is totally redundant. Merchants are already paying for processing, which means the Peak season fee is simply a duplicate charge.

In reality, the Peak season fee is a cash grab.

Year-end upgrade fee: Providers charge this fee to cover the costs associated with technological improvements or "modernization." Supposedly, this allows the provider to keep abreast of the competition and become more efficient. Even if such upgrades take place and they may or may not come under the heading of 'the cost of doing business.'

Such upgrades should be paid for out of the provider's profits, not by merchants paying additional fees. This is another example of a spurious fee. It sounds legitimate, but is phony.

PCI FEE: PCI is short for PCI DSS, which represents Payment Card Industry Data Security Standard. Essentially, the PCI fee is nothing more than an insurance fee that merchants pay against online hacking. It's an online fraud fee. There are two problems with PCI fees. One, online hacking is extremely rare. Two, the cost of compliance is nominal. Yet many ISOs charge merchants outrageous PCI compliance fees. The merchants pay because they are afraid. They don't know that the odds of ever being hacked are billions to one. "One ISO is charging all his merchants a $250 per merchant PCI compliance fee. With 5,000 merchants, that comes to $1.25 million - a lot of money to make based on people's emotions."[18]

What it comes down to is this: certain ISOs are simply leveraging merchants' fears to make money. PCI fees are cash grabs dressed up in haute couture. They look good, but under the high-fashion threads resides the same old flim-flam.

TERMINATION FEE: Also called a cancellation fee. The Termination fee is potentially the largest fee that any merchant will have to pay. What it boils down to is if a merchant wants to end his account early, a fee is charged. Typical merchant account contracts are 1 to 5 years in length, with the average being 3 years. Some providers charge merchants $150 to $300 to terminate prematurely, which is bad enough. Other providers, though, are downright reprehensible in their practices. If a merchant wants to cancel his account, the provider assesses all statement fees and monthly minimums remaining on the contract, along with a "lost profit" fee, which is based on an assumption of profits the provider would have earned during the full term of the contract. In other words, the merchant has to buy his way out of the contract. And the

---

18 'PCI Security and Compliance,' *USA Merchant Solutions*, June 24, 2010.

price of the buy out is the total amount due over the total duration of the contract.

Even a merchant that does not terminate his contract early is subject to questionable tactics by some providers. At the end of the contract cycle, there is a 30-day window in which the merchant may cancel. If the merchant does not cancel during that window, the contract automatically renews. And the entire burden of canceling the contract rests on the merchant. The provider does not inform the merchant that the contract is ending. Nor does the provider ask the merchant if he wishes to renew the contract. If the merchant does not educate himself as to the conditions of his contract, reading the fine print, he will find himself locked into another cycle willy nilly. If that occurs, and the merchant desires to terminate the contract, he will have to buy himself out.

According to Mr. X, "Early termination fees are wrong. They are insidious cash grabs."

And Mr. X should know. Back in 1999 he masterminded the Y2K fee, which is still talked about today. When industry insiders speak of the Y2K fee, they do so with awe in their voices. The Y2K fee was the granddaddy of fee-based cash grabs.

In 1999, everyone was afraid that when the 21st Century rolled around no purchases could be made with credit/debit cards. The terminals needed to be updated or they wouldn't accept transactions. Anyway, that was the story that went around and since there was, supposedly, considerable cost involved in updating the terminals and the systems they fed into, a Y2K fee was charged. Therefore, merchants were hit with a $100 Y2K fee.

Eighty-five percent of the merchants slammed with the Y2K fee paid it without even blinking. Those who didn't—the other 15%—picked up the phone and inquired about the $100 fee. They were told that it was an error. They didn't need to bother paying it.

Overnight, the merchant provider made millions of dollars.

The success of the Y2K fee opened the door for industry-wide fake fees. When the industry realized how easy it was to make money, grab the cash, by imposing fake fees, more and more fake fees began appearing. It was like watching a magic show in Las Vegas, where the magician kept pulling rabbits out of his hat. The sharp ISOs kept pulling fake fees out of their hats, producing specious fees for services that did not exist. It was cash-grab-city. And unsuspecting merchants paid the tab.

In 1999, a merchant decided to open a merchant account, so he could accept Visa/MasterCard payments for items sold through his online auction sales. He did due diligence, comparing many different merchant account services. In the end, he chose to go with Online Data Corporation, which ran out of the Chicago area. The merchant admitted that his choice was swayed by the fact that he found Online Data Corporation (ODC) through a site sponsored by Fran Tarkenton, the former NFL quarterback.

ODC's fees included a minimum $10 per month fee, a 30-cent per transaction fee, and an interchange percentage rate of 2.70%. In addition, there was a $49.95 per month fee—payable to Global Finance and Leasing—that provided a website with an integrated shopping cart. Global Finance and Leasing required the merchant to sign a two-year lease.

Before signing, the merchant carefully considered whether or not the agreement would benefit his business. He decided it would. So he opened the account.

Payments on his website were processed through Cybercash, and could be batched daily or weekly. Deposits appeared in his bank account within a few days of submittal. The merchant discovered that many of his customers used the Cybercash option, especially on more expensive items. Because he could accept Visa/MC and thus ship immediately, the merchant had an edge over his competitors. Business boomed.

Each month, just like clockwork, ODC charged his account the $10 minimum, along with any fees. Global Finance and Leasing charged his account $49.95 for the website and shopping cart.

The merchant was pleased with the smoothness of the entire operation. He felt he had made a savvy business decision.

Then things changed.

In December 1999, ODC charged him an additional $99. No explanation was given for the extra charge. Just $99. The merchant telephoned ODC's customer-service department and inquired about the fee. The service rep told him it was for "Y2K updates." She told him she would send a letter explaining the reasons for the charge. The letter must have gotten lost in the mail, because the merchant never received it.

The merchant felt the so-called Y2K updates were nonsensical. It wasn't his problem that their services needed updating. Yet the merchant paid the $99 fee. He didn't know what else to do.

A few months later, in April 2000, ODC's monthly minimum increased from $10 to $30, plus the interchange fee, and the lease charge of $49.95. In addition, the individual processing fee went from 30-cents to 40-cents per transaction. On the merchant's statement, ODC explained that the transaction fee had gone up because Cybercash had increased their fees. Hence, ODC had no choice but to pass the increase along to its merchants. No explanation was given as to why the monthly minimum had increased so dramatically.

In December 2000, another $99 fee was deducted from the merchant's bank account by ODC. Once again the merchant phoned ODC and asked what was going on. Why the $99 fee? He was informed that ODC now charged $99 per year for their service, an annual fee. Even though this fee was not part of the merchant's original agreement, it was now part of all new accounts. When the merchant pointed out that his account was not "new," he was told that this particular fee was retroactive and inclusive. In other words, everybody, new or old accounts, had to pay it.

By the middle of 2001, PayPal took over as the most popular form of online payment processing. Because his website did not have PayPal, the merchant's business began to decline. After about six months, business had fallen off so drastically that the merchant was paying more in fees each month than he was making. His account had gone from being a moneymaker to being a black hole, sucking the life out of his bank account.

The merchant called ODC and asked how to go about ending his account. What did the cancellation process entail? The service rep told him to fax his request for termination. However, his lease would continue for the term of the contract.

The merchant faxed in his request. Seven days later, ODC charged his account $195. Upset, the merchant once more called customer service. The rep told him that the $195 was an early termination fee, as per his contract. The merchant objected, saying that his contract said no such thing. Whereupon the rep was forced to locate the contract and examine it. After some hemming and hawing, the rep admitted the contract did not stipulate an early termination fee. However, the rep asserted that under the terms of the contract they could charge him for the full amount remaining on the contract, if they so chose. But they were being stand-up guys and only charging him a flat-fee of $195.

After further argument, the merchant realized ODC had him over a barrel. He could pay the $195 termination fee or buy himself out of the rest of the contract for close to $500. He paid the $195. In hindsight, he felt it was worth it just to be out of the contract and rid of ODC's shenanigans.

Obviously, Online Data Corporation's business model revolved around the tried and true shakedown called the cash grab. ODC raised its transaction fees by 200%, charged a $99 Y2K fee, and then initiated a $99 annual fee. In each instance, the merchant received no prior notice. Nor was the merchant given the option, under the 'changing circumstances', to opt out of his contract. ODC used the contract to bind the merchant to whimsical bogus fees, yet ODC did not feel bound to honor the original contract.

At best, ODC was unethical and at worst they were dishonest. This type of dishonesty is endemic to the credit card industry. It starts at the top, the card associations, and trickles downhill to the independent sales organizations and the merchant account providers.

Chapter 7
Discover Wars

Sears introduced the Discover Card in 1985. At the time, Sears was the largest retailer in the United States. Sears wanted to add an array of financial services to its existing customer services. This desire to expand its services stemmed from Sears' realization that although there was a lot of money to be made in retail sales, there was even more money to be made in finance. So the retailer purchased the Dean Witter Reynolds Organization, along with Coldwell, Banker & Company.

After these acquisitions, Sears began issuing its Discover Card. Discover Card's issuing bank was the Greenwood Trust Company, which was owned by Sears. Sears called its new financial services the Sears Financial Network. In effect, Sears was offering a one-stop financial service center in each of its stores. And because of Sears' sheer size and customer base, the Discover Card quickly gained acceptance.

However, there were some problems. The fact that Sears owned and promoted the Discover Card limited the card's potential. Other major retailers did not want to accept the Discover Card because doing so only fattened Sears, which was the competition. At the same time, Wal-Mart was becoming a major thorn in the side of Sears, and so-called 'category killers' such as Toys 'R' Us were eating into Sears' profits. By the late 1980s, the Sears Financial Network was beginning to sink under its own weight.

Another big problem adding to Sears' monetary headaches was the fact that Discover Card was isolated by its reluctance to utilize Independent Sales Organizations. In other words, Sears, in an attempt to protect its brand, had their own sales reps, who worked on salary, not on commission. Discover Card insisted on doing their own thing in their own way. Part of this insistence stemmed from Visa and MasterCard's exclusionary policies. Visa and MasterCard would not allow banks issuing Visa or MasterCard to simultaneously issue Discover Card.

Discover Card's small army of salaried sales reps were young and brash. Their salaries were not dependent on making sales to merchants, which meant they either didn't know how or weren't inclined to utilize the usual sales approach known as 'buff and polish.' Instead, they adopted Gestapo-like tactics. They waited until after the ISO reps had contacted local merchants, then they swooped down like buzzards on the merchants. Part of the Discover Card reps sales pitch involved speaking ill of Visa and MasterCard, along with bad mouthing the ISO sales reps as riff-raff intent on ripping off merchants.

The reps from Discover Card informed the hapless merchants that the ISO reps misrepresented their rates, fees and services in order to get the merchants to sign on the dotted line. Once the agreements were signed, all bets were off. The rates went up, the fees were exorbitant, and the promised services were never delivered. In other words, said the Discover Card reps, the ISOs sharks disguised as sheep. If, however, the merchants wanted to deal with straight shooters, who were not working on commission and thus were honest, the merchants should dump Visa and MasterCard and sign on with Discover Card.

Needless to say, Discover Card's tactics caused problems. Word of what was going on filtered back to the ISOs, whose reps earned their living off commissions. No commissions meant no food on the table, no rent, and no shoes on little Johnnie's feet. The ISO reps had no alternative. They retaliated. Initially, the retaliation consisted of verbal warnings to the Discover Card reps. The warnings went unheeded. Discover Card's reps kept right on trying to pull the carpet out from under the ISO's feet.

Finally, the ISOs had had enough. War was declared. The Discover War was on.

ISO reps and Discover Card reps actually fought physically. Fisticuffs took place. One of Ralph Fontana's reps was a former college football lineman. One day, the lineman confronted a Discover Card rep, who had just overturned a sale to a merchant. The merchant dropped

Visa and MasterCard and signed on with Discover Card. The lineman made accusatory remarks. The Discover Card rep replied heatedly. Angry words were exchanged. Then a boxing match began. Blows were exchanged. According to onlookers, the lineman literally pulverized the guy from Discover Card.

That wasn't all. Other ISO reps tailed Discover Card guys, learning what kind of cars they drove. When the Discover Card reps parked and walked away from their cars, the ISO reps moved in. Sauntering up to the reps' cars, they pulled out a bag of sugar and poured into the gas tanks of the cars. Later, when the Discover Card reps returned to their cars, they'd start them up and drive off. They'd get a mile or two before the engines seized up.

It wasn't nice. It was war. The Discover Wars.

The war continued for almost three years, 1988-1990.

Finally, Ralph Fontana had enough. He called Discover and complained about their tactics of bad mouthing the ISOs. Ralph's counterpart at Discover listened, but was non-committal. In effect, Discover told Ralph and the ISOs to kiss off.

About a month later, Fontana called Discover again. This time the person in charge was female. Her predecessor had gotten the axe, probably due to his attitude, which was that of total non-cooperation.

Ralph Fontana said, "The constant conflicts and bad mouthing needed to come to an end. This rough stuff isn't helping anyone."

The Discover rep agreed.

"What if we paid Discover referral fees?" asked Fontana. "We'll pay Discover a fixed-fee for every referral you send our way. That way both of us will benefit. And it will bring a halt to all the verbal ambushes. How does that sound?"

In other words, the ISOs would pay Discover a flat fee—called a "bird dog fee" —for every referral Discover threw to the ISOs.

She went for it. A quasi-state of peace replaced the all-out conflict of the Discover Wars.

As Fontana remarked, "Discover just never knew how to do business." As it turned out, Fontana's observation proved to be prescient.

Eventually, Sears had enough. Entering the realm of financial services had proven to be a mistake. In 1993, Sears sold off its financial network. Discover Card became part of the Dean Witter financial services firm. Up until this point, Sears' body of stores had only accepted its store credit cards and the Discover Card. On the one hand, this brand-protection strategy was understandable. Sears was hoping to carve out its own financial service kingdom. On the other hand, the strategy stemmed from an almost paranoid vision of the rapidly expanding world economic system, which was fast becoming a true global economy. In other words, by only accepting its own credit cards, Sears limited its own growth.

Once Sears saw the handwriting on the wall, they dumped the kingdom idea and began accepting MasterCard and Visa, along with its store credit card and Discover Card.

In 1997, Dean Witter united with Morgan Stanley. Greenwood Trust changed names in 2000, becoming Discover Bank. Throughout all these shifts and changes, one thing didn't change. Discover Card was still at war with Visa and MasterCard. In 2004, the Supreme Court decided that the exclusionary policy of Visa and MasterCard, not allowing Visa/MasterCard member banks to issue Discover Cards, was just that, exclusionary. Within days of the Supreme Court's decision, Discover Card filed suit in federal court against Visa and MasterCard. Among other things, the suit sought monetary damages from Visa and MasterCard.

At almost the same time, Discover made a deal with GE Consumer Finance, which issued three cards for Wal-Mart and its wholesale warehouse stores, called Sam's Club. GE bank agreed to issue Discover Cards. GE bank also agreed to process its credit card transactions, both Wal-Mart cards and Discover Cards, through the Discover Network. This meant that all of a sudden Discover Card had an ally in its ongoing wars. Wal-Mart was a powerful ally. Yet Wal-Mart was guilty of the same kind of brand-protectionist thinking as Discover Card. And it wasn't until two years later, in 2006, that Wal-Mart finally saw the handwriting on the wall. Wal-Mart began accepting MasterCard for purchases in its Sam's Clubs stores.

Then in 2005, as part of its campaign against Visa and MasterCard, Discover Card purchased PULSE, which was an electronic fund transfer association. This move allowed Discover Card to begin issuing debit and ATM cards.

While all this strategic maneuvering was going on, Morgan Stanley considered selling its Discover Card holdings. After much discussion, Morgan Stanley decided to spin off Discover Financial Services. A public announcement was made to the effect that in six months Discover Financial Services would be an independent company. Two months later, Morgan Stanley changed its mind. Only not wanting to admit to anything as crass as vacillation, Morgan Stanley declared they were 'reassessing' their options.

Reassessment led Morgan Stanley to a new conclusion. The company would not sell Discover Financial Services. However, 16 months later, in December of 2006, Morgan Stanley changed its collective mind once again. The company re-announced its intention to spin off Discover Financial Services as an independent company. This time, Morgan Stanley actually followed through. In June of 2007, Discover Financial Services became its own boss.

Despite Morgan Stanley's irresolution, the war continued. In fact, it had never abated.

Seeking new horizons, new financial territories to conquer, Discover Card turned its gaze toward China, whose economy was growing in leaps and bounds. In 2005, the Discover Network hooked up with China UnionPay Network (CUP). The CUP network agreed to accept Discover Cards at UnionPay ATMs and point-of-sale terminals in China. In return, the PULSE network would accept CUP cards in the United States. This coup made Discover Card the most widely accepted U.S. credit card in China. Thus, Visa, MasterCard, and American Express were forced into playing underling roles.

In Europe, Discover Card had issued credit cards in the United Kingdom since 1999. One card bore the Morgan Stanley brand, while the other bore the Goldfish brand, which Discover Card had purchased from Lloyd's TSB in

2005. By 2006, Discover had hooked up with LINK, which was an ATM network in the United Kingdom. Under the reciprocal agreement, access to over 300,000 cash machines in the U.S. and the U.K. became available to card members. Then in 2008, Discover sold the whole thing to Barclays, which proceeded to re-brand the two cards as Barclaycard Goldfish and Barclaycard Platinum.

In another 2008 move, Discover Financial Services bought out the Diners Club network. CitiBank let the network go for $165 million. Outside the United States, the Diners Club network was considered a major network, especially in Europe and South America. This purchase allowed Discover Financial Services to merge the Discover Network with the Diners Club network. The result was an international network, processing transactions from Discover Cards and Diners Club cards.

Frank X. McNamara's original credit card idea, which he called Diners Club, and which began with twenty-two restaurants and one hotel, was still alive and well. It was international in scope.

No More Cards

Discover Card's war keeps on keeping on. In 2010, AT&T, Verizon, and T-Mobile teamed up with Discover and Barclays to test a new NFC payment system. NFC is 'near field communication,' which allows the exchange of information via radio frequency at a distance of about 4 inches.

What's important here is that the enemy, or in more socially acceptable terms the 'competitor,' of this venture is Visa and MasterCard. Discover Card wants to re-invent the credit card industry. They want to own the consumer. Anything purchased by any consumer will be purchased using their system, if Discover has their way.

If NFC payments gain acceptability, most, if not all, businesses will have a cash register to support hard currency purchases, along with Visa and MasterCard terminals, and now a NFC reader. The estimated cost of the reader is $200.

In San Francisco, Bling Nation has hooked up with PayPal. PayPal handles payment processing, while Bling provides tags or stickers, which are attached to the backs of cell phones. The stickers are wireless data transmitters.

It works like this: the smart phone user taps the Bling sticker on a proprietary reader at the retailer. The reader pulls money from the users PayPal account. Security for the transaction is the same as it ever was. Users are required to enter a personal identification number (PIN) for purchases. However, instead of entering the PIN into a terminal or into the reader, the PIN is entered into the smart phone.

Merchants purchase or lease the readers, which is another expense. But the good part is that the complicated, confusing and exorbitant tiered system of Interchange fees is—as it stands right now in the testing phase—done away with. Merchants are charged a flat-rate fee of 1.5% of the total of every transaction, which is much less than the average transaction rate for accepting plastic credit cards. In addition, merchants receive almost instantaneous feedback about their customers' spending habits. In other words, merchants can analyze data and target regular customers with special offers, such as sales or coupons.

David Greene, owner of Live Greene in Menlo, California, likes the NFC system. "I love that the transaction fees are less than credit cards. It's lowering transaction costs, which means it's boosting my profits."

PayPal's goal is to become the number one payment processor for mobile payments, bumping Visa, MasterCard, AmEx, and Discover Card into second place. To that end, PayPal has come up with mobile applications for Apple's iPhone and Android-based smart phones, using 'bump' technology that allows consumers to make purchases by doing exactly what the word 'bump' implies. Scott Thompson, president of PayPal, said, "We aspire to be the best way to pay and be paid."

Rumor has it that Apple is planning to provide a similar service with its next generation iPhone, iPad, and iPod. Apple Inc. recently brought on board Benjamin Vigier, who will head up Apple's mobile commerce division. Vigier has lots of experience in Near Field Communication, having worked at mFoundry and SanDisk Corporation.

According to Richard Doherty, director of the consulting firm Envisioneering Group, Apple will begin mobile payment services sometime near the middle or end of 2011, combining it with iTunes and adding loyalty credits and points to the service. Supposedly, according to Doherty, Apple has a prototype payment terminal ready to go. In an effort to give the launch a shot in the arm the terminal will probably be heavily subsidized or provide for free to small businesses.

Apple's goal is to transform the iPhone, the iPad, and the iPod into digital wallets. If the transformation is successful, potential revenues for Apple are estimated in the billions.

The competition is not lollygagging. Sonim Technologies announced it would add NFC to its XP3300 Force device in 2011. In May 2011, Research In Motion (RIM) stated it would unveil the Blackberry Bold 9900, which will boast NFC technology. And of course, Google announced that smart devices utilizing its Android operating system would contain Google Wallet, allowing users to make NFC transactions.

Meanwhile, according to industry insiders, Discover Card and its partners are conducting pilot testing of wireless payment chips embedded in phones in four large metropolitan cities in the U.S. Yet Discover's war with Visa and MasterCard isn't over, as both Visa and MasterCard have conducted mobile payment pilots of their own. And most industry analysts say Visa and MasterCard are well positioned to form alliances with mobile carriers and/or smart phone manufacturers.

The fact that Discover hooked up with Barclays confuses some analysts. On the positive side, Barclays has already done much testing of NFC based payments in the United Kingdom. On the negative side, Barclays remains a British company with little or no brand recognition in the U.S. This lack of brand recognition implies a trust issue in the minds of American consumers, who don't have any faith in a brand they haven't heard of before.

At the same time, while all this NFC testing and jockeying for position is going on, other companies, such as Intuit Inc., Square, and VeriFone Systems have taken a different approach. They have designed applications that enable smart phones to read traditional credit cards. This system involves 'swiping' the card along a reader built into the smart phone.

At stake for all these companies is billions of dollars. And since NFC is a standard, for the consumer it's simply a matter of reprogramming a little chip inside the phone. For the credit card companies and the payment processing companies, it's more complicated. The winning company will be the one that not only gets there first, but that also gains recognition as "most acceptable."

Since there are over 1 billion credit/debit cards in the wallets and purses of Americans, that means every man, woman, and child has an average of three cards. If the Discover-AT&T-Verizon-T-Mobile consortium proves to be the most acceptable, Discover may well win the payment processing war.

Before victory can be declared, a few obstacles must be overcome. First, people—consumers—don't like change. So the challenge is getting consumers to feel comfortable with making purchases in a new way. The second problem is security issues. If an individual loses or misplaces his phone or his phone is stolen, his bank account is at risk. Plus, Near Field Communication signals are easy to pirate, which would more than likely lead to increased fraud and thievery. The third problem is the easiest to remedy. Most merchants don't have NFC readers. Readers would have to be placed in millions of retail outlets.

If all these issues can be resolved, and if NFC mobile payments take off, the ISOs may get a new lease on life.

NFC mobile payment systems, which are also called 'virtual' payment systems, according to Ralph Fontana, will probably take off and become a big hit with consumers. Why? As Ralph said, "Anything technology-driven, especially with young people, has unlimited potential in today's world."

From the merchants' viewpoint, virtual payment has one strong advantage: the merchant pays no fees. There is a transaction fee, but that fee is passed on to the consumer, who, in most cases, doesn't even realize he/she is paying the fee. And if he does realize it, he doesn't care.

Not only is the fee negligible, 1.5%, but most modern consumers simply figure that's the price of convenience. Convenience is a luxury consumers are willing to pay for.

On the other hand, payment systems such as PayPal, which as yet is not a NFC payment system, but soon will be (testing is ongoing), are not sophisticated enough for retailers. PayPal does not work like Visa and MasterCard. Upon careful examination, PayPal makes use of factoring, which is forbidden by the card associations. Factoring is where one merchant accepts a credit card payment for another merchant. This practice opens the door to fraud and frequent chargebacks, which probably explains PayPal's return policy. A policy that merchants feel punishes the seller.

PayPal may work for individual buyers and sellers on EBay, but for the vast majority of retailers PayPal is a rip off. Smaller, lower volume merchants pay 2.99%, along with a 35-cent transaction fee on each and every transaction. High-volume merchants pay only 1.99%, which makes PayPal attractive. PayPal can offer low rates to high-volume merchants because PayPal allows buyers to pay three different ways: from their accounts, a linked bank account, or credit card. No matter how the customer pays, PayPal charges a fee to both buyers and sellers. In other words, both sides of the transaction end up paying a fee. Payments from PayPal accounts carry no cost to PayPal, which means high-profit to PayPal on such transactions. PayPal uses those profits to subsidize its credit card processing costs by offering low processing fees to high-volume merchants.

Another obstacle confronting PayPal is marketing. PayPal has none. The company has not sold itself and its fee structure as "the price of convenience." Therefore, consumers don't recognize PayPal as a quick and easy way to do business. And smaller and medium-sized merchants won't 'buy it' because PayPal's transaction fee is 3%. In addition, PayPal has vast potential security problems. Listing a credit card or linking a bank account with a payment system that every hacker in the world in trying to break into is risky.

Essentially, if it weren't for the popularity of EBay, PayPal would already have gone the way of the dinosaurs.

Chapter 8
Swimming With Sharks

Possibly the scariest movie of all time is *Jaws*. After seeing the movie, many people refused to swim in the ocean. They decided they had no desire to be shark bait. There are, however, sharks that swim on land. Jimmy Buffet sang about them in one of his popular songs. Sharks that swim on land are unscrupulous individuals, looking to take advantage of the unsuspecting. Sometimes ISO sales reps resemble the twenty-five foot shark in *Jaws*. When they come across an unsuspecting merchant, they attack. Such sales reps don't draw blood or bite off arms and legs. Instead, they sign the merchants to contracts, which turn out to be very, very expensive.

Merchants can ward off such attacks by means of shark repellant. The best shark repellant in the world is knowledge. By knowing where the sharks are and how they approach, merchants can avoid becoming shark bait. To that end, Ralph Fontana suggests that merchants be aware of the following devious sales practices.

TERMINALS: Terminals may be either leased or purchased. A new terminal, depending on the type of terminal, costs as little as $295. Others cost $500 to $700. Leasing a terminal involves paying a set monthly fee, along with tax and insurance over the length of the contract. So a merchant signing a 48-month lease at $119 per month ends up paying $5,700 for the terminal. The merchant could have saved $5,000 by simply purchasing the terminal.

Some businesses prefer to lease because they want the newest equipment and the service that accompanies it. Any business choosing to lease should be able to get a terminal for $29 to $49 per month. And don't forget to cancel the lease at the end of the contract. Otherwise, the unsuspecting merchant will find himself paying forever on the same terminal.

Free Terminals: Merchants should be immediately suspicious of any sales rep offering free terminals. Terminals are not free. In reality, free terminals turn out to be loaners, and then only for as long as you remain with the processor. Even then, there is sure to be a minimum requirement on rates, monthly fees, monthly minimums, and other assorted fixed fees. If the merchant chooses to change processors, the loaner must be returned within 10 days. And the loaner must be in pristine condition. If both requirements are not met, the merchant's checking account will be charged for the full amount specified on the contract.

Fees: Payment processors have more than 40 different types of fees. Most merchants are unaware of this. Merchants tend to focus on the interchange rate quoted by the sales rep. If the rate is lower than the merchants currently pay, they think they've gotten a good deal. The reality is that merchants always pay more than the contracted rate. The actual amount the merchants pay is called the 'effective rate.' The effective rate includes the interchange rate and all other fees. Merchants can discover their effective rate by adding up all of the fees on their monthly statements. The total amount is then divided by the credit card net sales on the same statement. The resulting number is then multiplied by 100. This is the effective rate.

PCI-DSS Compliance: PCI refers to Payment Card Industry. DSS refers to Data Security Standards. Together the terms refer to security measures designed to prevent theft of credit card information. These security measures are constantly being updated and improved. Many devious sales reps try to get merchants to replace their terminals by stating that the merchants' current terminals are not PCI-DSS compliant. Repelling this type of attack is simple. Merchants can easily verify whether or not their equipment is compliant. At no time should merchants tolerate high-pressure tactics from sales reps.

Contract Changes: Since most sales reps are independent, they cannot make any changes in the processing contract. If they do make changes, the processor has no responsibility to honor them. Processing contracts specifically state that changes are prohibited. Devious sales reps will make changes in the contract in order to get a merchant to sign. Once the merchant signs, the sales rep will transmit only the completed and signed portions of the contract. The processing company will have no idea that any changes were ever agreed to.

Processor Calls for Information: Most merchants do not know who their processor is. They only know whom their sales rep is. So when the unsuspecting merchant gets a call, saying, "This is your processor and we need some information from you," the merchant provides the information. According to Ralph Fontana, this is a scam. The caller is seeking information to use on a new processing contract.

A merchant's processing company already has the information they require. If any other information becomes necessary, the processor will have the merchant's sales rep contact him.

Lower Rate: The first question most merchants ask a sales rep is, "What is the lowest rate I can get?" A devious sales rep will say, "0% or 1.39%. Zero percent, of course, is a bald-faced lie. There is no such thing as a 0% rate. And the 1.39% rate is only for swiped debit cards. Which means that most cards accepted by the merchant will not qualify for that rate. In fact, most transactions will automatically default to a much higher rate. In other words, any sales rep who quotes an extraordinarily low rate is more than likely scamming the merchant.

Affiliated With Visa and MasterCard: Sales reps claiming to work directly for Visa and MasterCard are lying flimflammers. First, Visa and MasterCard are separate entities. Second, Visa and MasterCard do not issue cards. Third, Visa and MasterCard do not process cards. Only Member Banks are allowed to issue and process credit cards. Processing companies are registered with the card associations and sponsored by Member Banks. All registered processors pay the same Interchange fees and Assessments. The registered processor then set pricing based on the Interchange fees and Assessments, which explains why merchants receive different quotes from different processors.

FLAT RATE FOR ALL TRANSACTIONS: Ralph Fontana asserts that this scam usually turns out to be one of the most expensive for merchants. The sales rep tells the merchant that his company offers a single flat rate for all transactions. Quoted rates vary from 0.75% to 1.69%. The unsuspecting merchant likes the sound of those numbers as much as he likes the idea of a "flat rate." So the merchant signs the contract. In reality, the merchant has just signed an Interchange Plus contract. Only this contract will hit the merchant with charges 8 times higher than the normal Interchange Plus contract. A normal Interchange Plus contract charges the merchant a markup of .20% to .35%. The contract the devious sales rep is presenting is charging a markup of 1.69%. In other words, the unsuspecting merchant has just agreed to pay a flat rate of 1.69% in addition to the regular Interchange rate.

BLANK CONTRACTS: It is hard to imagine, but merchants actually fall for this scam. It goes like this. The devious sales rep informs the merchant that he can save the merchant a lot of money. The sales rep presents very attractive rates. The merchant realizes he could save a lot of money. So the merchant is eager to sign. The sales rep pulls out a contract and says, "Just sign this blank contract and I'll fill in the numbers we talked about later." The gullible merchant signs. And the sales rep fills in much higher numbers than discussed. For the merchant, the contract is binding. He pays.

CHURNING: Churning takes place when a sales rep for Bob's processing company changes jobs. He leaves Bob's and goes to work for Fred's processing company. Fred's processing company gives sales reps bonus payments for new processing contracts. So the sales goes to the merchants he signed up while working at Bob's, re-signing them contracts with Fred's. For each re-signing the sales rep receives $1,000. Easy money.

The merchants re sign because, like most people, they prefer a familiar face, someone they know. What the merchants forget is the early termination fee (ETF) clause in their contracts. By re-signing, merchants often end up paying enormous amounts of money in the form of ETFs.

Some business owners look to their bank for credit card processing. These merchants typically believe that all processors are the same. Thus, they reason that their bank will treat them better to retain their business. Unfortunately, this isn't always the case. Banks provide merchant services believing such services will keep merchants from switching banks. In other words, banks use merchant services as ropes, hoping to tie merchants to the mother ship. Eventually, of course, the merchant is so closely moored to the bank that it would be inconvenient to leave. Which is just what the bank wants, because then the bank can charge higher rates and fees for the convenience it provides.

Since most banks use third-party processors, merchants usually end up paying more by using their banks than by simply signing on with a processor. Most banks are publicly owned, for profit entities. They build in profit by creating new fees. By using their bank, merchants pay fees to the bank and fees to the bank's processing company. It's almost a double-dose of fees.

The largest processors include First Data, Bank of America Merchant Services, Chase-Paymentech, Global, and Heartland Payment Services. Once again, since most merchants don't even know who their own processor is, these big-name providers go unrecognized by all but a few merchants. Big-name providers are, as the designation implies, big. Which means they have sales agents to sell their services and a customer service department to service the accounts sold by the agents. Many merchants find this arrangement distasteful. Every time the merchant has a question or a problem, he ends up dealing with a different customer service agent. There is no consistency, no familiarity, no sense of the 'personal touch,' no name or face recognition.

Studies have shown that it is more expensive for processors to gain new customers than it is to retain existing customers through good service. In addition, the same studies indicate that retaining clients through superior service actually gains more new clients because of word-of-mouth referrals.

Thus, when it comes to payment processing bigger is not always better.

Independent sales organizations (ISOs), although smaller than the big-name providers, can often provide fair rates and excellent service. ISOs have lower overhead than banks or big-name providers, which means they can offer more reasonable costs. And their customer service is more personal.

There is an old adage that says, “You get what you pay for.” Merchants need to remember this adage when signing with a sales rep. For example, Bathing Ape is an extremely popular brand of clothing among the rich and famous. Bathing Ape hoodies retail for $300 to $800, depending on the style. And Bathing Ape shoes go for $189. Yet one can go online and purchase, supposedly, a pair of Bathing Ape shoes for $49. What a deal! However, the truth of the matter is that the buyer is not getting what he wants for $49. He is getting cheap knock-offs.

The point is this: each merchant needs to decide what level of service he desires, and how much he is willing to pay for what he wants. Ultimately, merchants are in business to make a profit, as are ISOs. Credit card processing companies expend time and money becoming registered credit card processors: bank sponsorship, registration fees, and financial backing just to name a few. Other expenses include computer security, customer service, technical support, office space, utilities, etc.

Processing companies utilize ISOs because by doing so they avoid paying salaries, unemployment expenses, and medical benefits. Plus, they don’t have the headache and paperwork involved in withholding taxes. In other words, ISOs are paid only for what they produce, and the sales reps are responsible for all costs associated with signing merchants.

On their part, ISOs are not limited in how much they can earn. If they sign up lots of merchants, they make lots of money. But they do have to work hard to make their money. They find and meet with potential merchants, set up equipment, provide training, and service existing merchants.

ISOs make money on equipment sales, by reprogramming existing equipment, application fees, leasing fees, and, in some cases, contract bonuses. Equipment sales include Internet gateways, terminals, wireless equipment, and point of sale systems.

Interchange fees go to the card associations, such as Visa and MasterCard. ISOs only make a profit on whatever they charge over and above the set interchange fee. For example, Visa's tiered interchange base rate is 2%. Fred's processing company sets their base rate at 2.19%. The processor (Fred's) and the sales rep split the profit of .19%.

With Interchange Plus pricing, Fred's processing company offers sales reps true Interchange rates. The 'Plus' is the mark up added by the sales rep. This 'Plus' is the sales rep's profit, which is split between the processor and the sales rep.

Monthly statement fees average $10 to $15 per month. If a sales rep offers a merchant lower statement fees, the merchant can rest assured that the sales rep is not sacrificing anything. The sales rep will more than make up the difference in surcharges for Mid-Qualified and Non-Qualified transactions.

Chapter 9
The Inquisition

Before any merchant decides to sign with a sales rep, he should take the time to ask a number of basic questions. The first question the merchant should ask is directed toward himself. What services does the merchant want from his processor? The merchant can discover the answer to this question very simply by considering how he prices his product and what services he offers to his customers.

Most businesses do not advertise that they are the cheapest. Customers regard such advertising to mean that the business offers no guarantees, does not stand behind its product, and does not provide any type of service. This is not what most customers want. In fact, marketing studies demonstrate that most customers desire quality service, along with quality products. And they are willing to pay for it.

The only instance where cheapest price wins is when everything else is equal. In other words, if all hardware stores offer the same level of service, the same convenience, and the same brands, then the store with the lowest price will win. But if one store offers superb service from knowledgeable sales people, and sells high-quality merchandise, then the equation changes. By offering services that its competitors cannot or will not offer, that one store will not lose customers on price alone.

Merchants should look at credit card processors the same way. There are hundreds of credit card processors. If the merchant's processor offers no special services, then why should the merchant give the processor his business?

Merchants accept credit cards to increase sales. Not only is the merchant providing a convenience, which brings in more customers, but credit card customers are more likely to make impulse purchases. Visa performed a study that indicated merchant sales increased by 56% when the merchant accepted credit cards. And MasterCard projected that 20% to 30% of credit card customers 'bought up,' that is, customers using credit cards bought more expensive items than customers not using credit cards.

Many merchants despise paying credit card fees. They believe they are being ripped off. In some cases they are, especially if they don't educate themselves and avoid dealing with unscrupulous sales reps and/or processors. Trying to avoid the pitfalls of credit card processing fees is a little like trying to walk through a minefield without setting off an explosion. To accomplish this task, a map pinpointing the locations of the mines is invaluable. Ralph Fontana, the dynamic maestro of industry insiders, suggests that merchants ask sales reps the following questions. By doing so, merchants can dodge tripping any mines.

1. Do you have contracts? And for how long?

Answer: all processors use contracts, which vary in length from 1 year to multiple years. The industry average is 3 to 5 years.

2. Do you have an early termination fee? If so, what is your early termination fee?

Answer: 95% of processors have early termination fees. Sometimes, processors will waive the early termination fees. Early termination fees vary from processor to processor. Some processors charge a flat rate early termination fee of $250. Other processors charge exorbitant early termination fees. In such instances, typically, merchants end up buying themselves out of the remaining portion of their contract. If the merchant operates a successful business, the early termination fee can be extremely costly.

3. What are my rates? Are there any transaction fees? Will my rates go up?

Answer: The merchants' rates depend on whether the merchant is hooked to tiered pricing or Interchange Plus. According to Ralph Fontana, most merchants will save money by signing up for Interchange Plus. All processors have transaction fees. Without transaction fees, processors would not make a profit.

The rates always go up. The card associations issue new rates every six months.

4. How long does it take me to get my money?

Answer: With some banks, merchants receive their money the next day. With processors, there is often a time lag of 24 to 48 hours before the merchants receive funds. Merchants who operate on a very low margin, and thus need their funds immediately, should be sure to find out what the turnaround time is. It can make the difference between remaining in business or closing the doors.

5. Do you charge a statement fee?

Answer: Most processors do. Some statement fees are as low as $2.50 per month. Others are as high as $15 per month. The industry average is between $10 and $15. If the sales rep offers to waive the statement fee, the merchant should beware. Such an enticing offer usually indicates that the difference will be made up in an area the merchant won't notice.

6. Do I have to buy a new terminal? Is there a lease involved?

Answer: The leasing of terminals is not as common as it used to be. Most merchants are better off simply purchasing terminals. Likewise, most sales reps expect merchants to purchase new terminals, as sales reps earn a profit from each terminal sold. By purchasing new terminals from the sales rep, the merchant can often negotiate better terms. In addition, terminals purchased from the sales rep will be preprogrammed, which means there will be no downtime. If the merchant does not purchase new terminals from the sales rep, there will more than likely be reprogramming fees of $50 to $100.

However, if a merchant's old terminals are supported by the new processor, there is no reason to purchase new terminals.

7. Can I do my transactions on my computer? Can I look up my account online?

Answer: Yes.

8. Do I have to change banks?

Answer: No.

9. Can you bill me at the end of the month?

Answer: Sometimes processors will bill monthly, if asked to do so by the merchant. If the merchant operates a large company, processors are more likely to agree to monthly billing. Normally, most processors charge fees on a daily basis.

10. Will you pay for me to get out of my existing contract?

Answer: When merchants ask this question, they are usually referring to early termination fees. In other words, the merchant is asking if the new processor will pay the early termination fees associated with his old contract. According to Ralph Fontana, the new processor will pay for the merchant to get out of his existing contract, "if it makes sense."

The new processor will pay the fees, if he can make a profit by signing the merchant.

11. Do you have chargeback? How do they work?

Answer: According to Ralph Fontana, merchants rarely ask this question. And merchants who do ask the question are guilty of lots of chargebacks. All processors utilize chargeback fees, which are stipulated on the merchant's contract. The retrieval fee (request for documentation) is usually $15 to $20, with an additional $20 to $35 if the transaction is charged back, which is where the processor seizes money out of the merchant's account.

When a merchant is notified that a customer has contesting a transaction, merchants must respond with supporting documentation immediately. Failure to do so results in loss of privilege and an automatic chargeback - the processor will pull funds from the merchant's account.

12. Do you have any type of annual fee?

Answer: Some processors do, some processors don't. However, most processors do have an annual fee. The processor may waive annual fees, if the merchant is a tough negotiator.

Chapter 10
The Dotted Line

Once a merchant decides to accept credit cards, and has asked his sales rep the questions in Chapter 9, and has concluded the sales rep is not a scam artist, it is time to sign the processing agreement. Prior to signing on the dotted line, every merchant should be sure to get a full copy of the contract. Read it! And if necessary, pay a qualified contract attorney to review it.

Most processing agreements follow a similar template and contain the same stipulations and clauses. However, processing agreements are not standardized by any means, varying to one degree or another. Merchant processing agreements usually have four or five pages that stipulate pricing, followed by ten to twenty pages of terms and conditions. Anytime a dispute arises the processor will refer to and abide by the contract, which may be likened to the Ten Commandments written in stone.

The first portion of the typical processing agreement is the application, which asks for Business Information, such as corporate names, address, home office, business structure, and so forth. Included in this section is the designation Merchandise or Service Sold, which is simply what type of product(s) the merchant sells. The merchant will be asked to select a standard industrial classification code or merchant classification code. Selecting the proper code is important. For the code determines the Interchange rate for which the business qualifies, which determines what types of cards the merchant can accept.

The next section is called Monthly Bank Card Sales, which is the amount of credit card sales made each month by the merchant's business. Merchant's who guesstimate this number are shooting themselves in the foot. It is vital that the number be an accurate reflection of sales, as it determines the level of underwriting. Fudging on the low side may result in a cap assignment, which will limit the amount of credit card sales the business may transact each month. Fudging on the high side may result in the merchant's application being declined.

Average Ticket is the title of the next section. Average Ticket refers to the amount of the merchant's average transaction. Once again, this number should accurately reflect the average sales amount, because it too determines the level of underwriting. The higher the number, the higher the risk. For example, Joe's Tire Emporium and Sally's Candy Shoppe both do $50,000 worth of business every month.

Joe's average ticket is $400. Tires are expensive. Sally's average ticket is $5. Candy is cheap, but Sally sells a lot of it because many people have a sweet tooth. Joe's Tire Emporium is considered a higher risk because the potential loss for one transaction is 80 times higher than at Sally's Candy Shoppe.

The Highest Ticket section is also important for underwriting reasons. Merchants should plug in specific and accurate numbers.

The next section is Percentage Swiped, which refers to the percentage of sales done by swiped cards, the percentage of sales keyed with an imprint, and the percentage of sales keyed without an imprint. The three percentages must equal 100%. The risk on swiped cards is considered lower, which means swiped transactions carry a lower Interchange rate. Keyed transactions have a higher risk, and should be imprinted to negate the possibility of chargebacks. Transactions keyed in without an imprint refers to telephone, mail or Internet sales.

Sales Method refers to the percentage of swiped or keyed transactions. It determines risk, which in turn determines underwriting. Sales Method also determines Interchange rate. For example, Sally's Candy Shoppe does equal amounts of swiped and keyed transactions. Therefore, Sally has two accounts, one for swiped and one for keyed. Both accounts on a tiered pricing structure. Joe's Tire Emporium utilizes swiped transactions almost exclusively. Joe has one account, which is tied to

Interchange Plus rates, which means Joe's Tire Emporium gets lower rates.

The point is this: filling out the sections accurately can save the merchant money.

The Merchant Site Survey is completed by the sales rep.

Next up is the Pricing Schedule, which refers to the Interchange rate(s) the merchant will pay. Merchants need to review this section in its entirety. Unfortunately, most merchants tend to focus on the Qualified rate. This is a mistake. Mid-Qualifed and Non-Qualified are just as important, if not more important, as many transactions do not fit under the umbrellas of Qualified. Merchants should remember that Mid-Qualified and Non-Qualified are terms contrived by processors, and each processor defines them differently. Processors contrive the terms and then insert the categories into the tiered pricing schedule. MasterCard and Visa have over 400 Interchange levels. The Qualified level is very narrowly defined.

By paying attention to the entire Pricing Schedule, merchants will avoid being surprised when they receive their monthly statements.

Most merchants should not sign on for the next section, which is the Merchant Club. Being a member of a Merchant Club has no advantages, except perhaps for very large businesses, and is usually tantamount to a rip-off.

The next section is a questionnaire, Cardholder DataStorage Compliance, which is required for all processing accounts. In some instances, this questionnaire is separate, and not part of the application. Nevertheless, it should be filled out accurately.

It is imperative that merchants realize that the application is part of the contract. The fees and rates the merchant is obligated to pay are contained in the application. And there is a clause in the body of the contract declaring that by signing the contract, the merchant is asserting that all parts of the contract are true and accurate. In other words, the merchant is legally binding himself to the provided information.

The Contract: With certain minor variations, the typical processing agreement contains the following sections.

Introduction and Definitions: This section states that the merchant agrees to abide by the rules of the processor, and that the merchant will utilize said processor as exclusive provider of all credit card transactions.

Service: This section lists the credit card brands the processor agrees to process, along with debit card processors and networks. If applicable, this section will also describe EBT card networks.

Procedures: Here, the merchant agrees to also abide by the rules of the card brands (card associations). The rules of the card brands are not contained in the contract; otherwise the contract would be thousands of pages long. The location of each card brand's rules is provided.

The merchant, not the processor, will pay fees assessed by the card brands.

Payment Card Industry-Data Security Standards are included in the 'procedures' section. The merchant is responsible for complying with PCI-DSS standards. However, many processing agreements fail to discuss how this is accomplished or where to go for help.

When new, future rules are issued by the card brands or PCI-DSS, the merchant becomes immediately responsible to those rules, which are "binding as soon as they are released." What this means is that the merchant must adhere to any additional, future rules that are not in the contract and that he may not even be aware of. This clause may be likened to an arranged marriage. Two five year-old children, who have never met each other and are unaware of the other's existence, will be wed at a future date, as per contract.

Marketing: The merchant agrees to use card brand logos in advertising and marketing campaigns. This includes logos on storefront doors, windows, etc. When the merchant stops accepting card brands, the merchant must remove the logos.

Payment, Charges and Fees: The merchant agrees to pay all fees. Furthermore, the merchant agrees to pay any fines, arbitration costs, and penalties imposed by the card associations. Trying to block, prevent or preclude the processor from collecting fees is strictly forbidden. What this means is that if the merchant closes his checking account so the processor cannot collect fees, the merchant is automatically in violation of contract.

EQUIPMENT AND SUPPLIES: This clause covers equipment or software used to transmit credit card data.

FINANCIAL INFORMATION: The merchant consents to provide the processor with complete financial statements, including complete financial statements from co-owners, principals or partners. If the merchant fails to fulfill this obligation, the processor may seek legal redress (file a lawsuit). In addition, the merchant agrees to keep copies of all sales or credit card receipts for a specified period of time, usually three years.

BUSINESS CHANGES: The merchant will provide 60-day advance notice of any change in business, including sale or transfer of stock, assets or liquidation thereof. Essentially, this clause states that if Sally's Candy Shoppe decides to start selling candy online, the Shoppe will give the processor plenty of advance notice.

TRANSFERABILITY: The processing agreement may be assigned to a new business owner, if the processor approves. What this means is that if Joe wants to sell his tire business to Howard, and Howard wants to keep the processing agreement in place, the processor has to approve of the transfer. If the processor does not approve the transfer, Joe can still sell his business to Howard, but Howard will have to find a new processor.

WARRANTIES AND REPRESENTATIONS: The merchant agrees to operate his business in a lawful manner. Any transactions will represent "bonafide" sales to customers. Sale slips will accurately reflect each transaction. The merchant will abide by all federal, state, and local laws. The merchant will fulfill his obligations to customers, and try to resolve disputes to the customer's satisfaction. The merchant will not forge signatures on receipts. All transactions will follow the rules of the card brands.

Merchants will not take cash advances by running their personal credit card through their credit terminal. This practice is called 'factoring.' The card associations frown on factoring, which is punishable by a merchant's capability to accept credit cards.

The merchant consents to abide by all security measures set forth by the card associations and PCI-DSS.

And finally, the merchant asserts that all information on the application is complete and verifiable. In legal terms, this clause addresses 'strict liability.' Strict liability means that if even one of the conditions of the contract is violated, the merchant is in breach of contract. In other words, there is no wiggle room. The processing agreement demands total transparency of the merchant, but not of the processor.

Indemnity: This clause makes the merchant responsible for resolving any and all customer complaints. If any complaint is not resolved, the merchant is responsible for any losses, not the processor. Furthermore, the merchant agrees to pay or indemnify the processor for damages, fees and costs, if the processor should ever be sued.

Limitation of Liability: The processor assumes no responsibility for the merchant's inability to process transactions, including power outages, equipment failure or 'Acts of God.'

Term and Termination: The average processing agreement is for three years. Regardless of the length, the contract automatically renews unless the processor is notified in writing prior to the renewal date. And even then, the notification period is usually defined by a very narrow window. If the merchant misses the window of opportunity, the contract rolls over for another three years.

This section of the contract also stipulates the early termination fee, which may be anywhere between $0 and the full amount remaining on the contract, including the processor's expected profit from the account. In most cases, early termination fees must be paid within 10 days of cancellation.

On the other hand, the processor may cancel the contract at any time, for any reason, and without notification or penalty.

The only equalizing factor in this section is that if the processor or Member Bank violates the terms of the contract, the merchant may, if he chooses, cancel the contract within 30 days of the violation. But only if the breach is not remedied. In other words, if the processor violates the contract and then corrects the violation, the merchant cannot cancel. The only way the merchant can cancel, in this scenario, is if the processor violates the contract and does not try to correct the violation. Essentially, the processor can violate the contract and get away with it.

Chargebacks: This clause defines 'chargeback,' which is when the processor seizes money from the merchant's account because of a customer's refusal to pay or fraud. The merchant is liable for all chargebacks. The merchant also acknowledges that customer authorization does not guarantee payment.

The chargeback clause behooves the merchant to strictly follow the rules of credit card acceptance and documentation.

Reserve Account: If a merchant has a low credit score or operates a business considered 'risky' by the processor or has a history of frequent chargebacks, the processor may hold back a certain percentage of the merchant's money, placing the money in a reserve account. The money in the reserve account is used to cover chargebacks.

Amendments: Changes to the contract must be in writing, and acknowledged by signatures of both the processor and the merchant. Naturally, these changes would be made prior to the merchant signing the contract. However, it is interesting to note that the card associations or the processor may change the terms of the contract at any time. The card associations and the processor do have to give the merchant written notice of any changes. After the changes go into effect, if the merchant processes even one transaction after that date, then the merchant has accepted the changes willy nilly.

Waiver: The merchant should take particular note of this clause. No part of the contract is waived unless the waiver is in writing. Only the processor or the Member Bank may waive any portion of the contract, not the sales rep. Sales reps are not authorized to make any changes in the contract. In other words, the merchant must have a waiver signed by the processor or the Member Bank before the waiver is binding.

Exchange of Information: The word exchange implies two parties participating equally. Not here. This clause is a one-way street. For here, the merchant agrees that the processor or Member Bank may run the merchant's credit report at any time.

General: This clause is a doozy. It states that if any provision of the contract is determined to be unenforceable, the rest of the contract remains intact and enforceable. In other words, processing agreements are literally written in stone.

Notices: This section defines how notices will be sent and when they become effective.

Agreement: This clause states that the contract authorizes the entire agreement. The contract supersedes all other agreements, whether oral or in writing. In other words, no matter what promises or representations the sales rep makes, none of it is binding.

Legal Waiver: Here, the merchant waives his right to trial by jury. This clause also precludes and prevents class-action lawsuits against processors or Member Banks or the card associations. The laws of the processor's home state, not the merchant's home state, dictate the interpretation of the contract. In case of court action, jurisdiction is granted to the home county of the processor.

This clause is a blatant attempt to pre-empt legal action by the merchant against the processor or Member Bank.

Effective Date: The effective date is not necessarily the date the merchant signs the contract. The effective date refers to the date the contract is accepted by the processor and the Member Bank.

Designation of Depository: The bank utilized by the merchant to receive deposits from the processor and make payments to the processor.

Financial Accommodation: This clause liberates the processor and the Member Bank from the contract, if the merchant goes bankrupt. However, if the reverse happens, the processor goes bankrupt, the merchant is not excused from the contract. Further, if the processor is not PCI compliant and the processor's database is compromised, the merchant is not permitted to absolve the contract.

Debit/ATM: The merchant must abide by the debit companies' rules and regulations. The processor merely provides access to the debit network. Other than that, the processor assumes no responsibility.

Electronic Benefit Transaction (EBT): EBT refers to food stamps. The processor provides access to the network, nothing more. Merchants are required to follow the rules of their home state.

Marks: This section gives guidelines on the proper use of logos and trademarks.

Mid-Qualified and Non-Qualified Surcharges/Cross-Border Fees: Merchants should read this clause carefully. The rate listed herein applies only to Qualified transactions. Any transaction that is not classified as Qualified becomes liable to Mid-Qualified and Non-Qualified rates, which are higher than the listed Qualified rate. Merchants be aware that the processor determines which transactions are Qualified and which are not.

Included in this section is an explanation of surcharges that may be applied to foreign cards.

Press Release: The processor retains the right to use the merchant's business in advertising campaigns.

Employee Actions: This is another of those one-way street clauses, which explicitly declares that the merchant is responsible for the actions of its employees. At the same time, the contract specifically declares that the processor is not responsible for the actions of its employees or independent sales reps.

Payment processing agreements, obviously, are not fair and balanced legal agreements. They are one-sided and problematic for merchants. For example, the agreement demands strict adherence to the rules of the card associations, Visa, MasterCard, Discover, and American Express. Yet the rules are not part of the contract. The contract tells where to find the rules for each card association. The rules are posted online.

The problem is that most merchants do not read the rules. MasterCard's regulations encompass 353 pages, while Visa's, by comparison, is a mere 141 pages. Merchants do not have time to plow through 353 pages of complicated information that, even if they did bother, is almost incomprehensible. Yet by signing the contract, merchants are pledging to follow the rules, rules they don't understand. And because they don't understand the rules, merchants are opening themselves up to expensive fines. If, for example, a merchant requires a minimum purchase or cardholder identification to use a credit card, the card association may impose a $20,000 penalty for the first offense.[19] All the cardholder has to do is complain to Visa or MasterCard. Visa or MasterCard will hit the processor with the fine, and the processor will pass the fine along to the merchant. Because remember, the merchant pledged to abide by the rules.

Another problematic clause in the processing agreement is Terms and Terminations. Most merchants don't bother reading the contract. Then, when they decide to switch processors because they feel they can get a better deal elsewhere; they are slammed with horrendous early termination fees.

Two clauses in most processing agreements give unethical sales reps 007 status: a license to lie, lie, lie. The first of these two clauses declares that the contract makes up the entire agreement, and that the contract supersedes all other oral or written representations. The second clause makes it very clear that only the Member Bank may alter the contract. Unscrupulous sales reps are aware of these clauses and use them to their advantage. They promise special rates and/or cross-out sections of the contract to get the merchants' signatures. Yet the promises and the changes are unsustainable because the sales reps do not have the authority to make promises or changes in the contract, and, if they do, they are not held responsible.

Merchants can avoid getting trapped in the web of lies by simply reading through the processing contract as presented. What it says is what it means. Either accept it or reject it as it stands.

The biggest mistake most merchants make is this: merchants believe the rate the sales rep quotes embraces all transactions. In tiered pricing, only Qualified

19 As of 2010, merchants are allowed to require a minimum purchase of $10 of customers wishing to use a credit/debit card.

transactions receive the lowest rate. All other transactions, Mid-Qualified and Non-Qualified, will carry significantly higher rates. The only exception is Interchange Plus pricing.

In the final analysis, merchants must read through their processing agreements before signing them. Merchant must understand each and every clause. In addition, merchants must read through and gain a working knowledge of the rules and regulations of the card associations. Failure to do so may result in bankruptcy or the inability to process credit card transactions.

Chapter 11
The Rules

Sally, of Sally's Candy Shoppe, is a smart merchant. She read through her processing agreement. She even had her attorney review it. After discussing the agreement with her attorney, Sally decided she would sign it. But only after reading through the rules and regulations of the card associations. She wanted to be sure she understood what she's getting into.

Sally went online and downloaded the rules from Visa, MasterCard and Discover, the three cards she would be accepting. She had decided against accepting American Express for two reasons: one, she had heard too many horror stories from other merchants and, two; she thought American Express charged exorbitant rates. Besides which she figured that people who carried AmEx cards also carried either a Visa or MasterCard. Thus, by refusing AmEx, Sally didn't believe she would be losing any business.

Sally spent two weeks reading and re-reading the rules. When she had a question, she called her sales rep and asked for clarification. Since her sales rep was honest, she got good answers. Once she understood what was expected of her as a merchant, Sally signed the processing agreement.

Sally's Candy Shoppe was open for business and business boomed. Sally had a good location and provided personalized service. She guaranteed her product, which was extremely tasty, and did targeted marketing and advertising. Moreover, Sally hired intelligent employees, whom she paid well. Sally also provided intense training for her employees in the area of service. Superior service and superior sweets were her mantra. These two qualities would keep the customers coming back.

And they did. Sally's Candy Shoppe swarmed with customers. For Sally not only offered yummy treats, but Sally's Candy Shoppe projected a certain ambiance, the ambiance of cool. Sally's was a place where people could satisfy their craving for something sweet and be seen. Being seen at Sally's carried social cachet.

Pretty soon, the candy store was so busy Sally had to add more employees. Things were humming.

Then things started to go wrong. Her employees began making errors. Not service related errors, but errors at the cash register: the point of sale. Credit card transactions were being mishandled. Sally became irritated. She held a mandatory meeting for her employees, where she exhorted them to do better. Exhortation didn't work. Transactions continued to be messed up. Fuming with exasperation, Sally tried to be patient with her employees, but everyone knew something was wrong. Sally emanated a black anger that she couldn't disguise. She either snapped at employees or spoke words dripping with caustic sarcasm. Soon, Sally's employees became defensive. They looked over their shoulders to see where Sally was, if she was watching them. They glared at customers, sighing impatiently, as they tried to move people along, get their money and get them out the door.

Business dropped off. The ambiance of Sally's Candy Shoppe went from cool to strained. People felt uncomfortable when they walked in the place. They felt unwelcome.

Sally was at her wit's end. Nervous, upset, and confused, she was popping Tums like candy. She didn't know what to do. If business kept falling off, she'd have to file for bankruptcy. Sally's Candy Shoppe would be just one more failed business.

One day in the Shoppe, Sally overheard one of her employees complaining to a fellow-worker. Both were young, female college students, who had worked for Sally since day one. One of the young ladies was blonde. The other was brunette. They were discussing how to void a transaction. "I don't know how to do it," said the brunette. "No one ever taught me. That's why I asked you to help me."

"I don't know either," said the blonde, shrugging.

The Apostle Paul came face to face with a blinding vision on the road to Damascus. Sally came face to face with a realization in a candy store. Sally realized she had made a mistake: a big one. She had emphasized the importance of personalized service to her employees. But she had not given them adequate training as cashiers.

Sally immediately contacted her sales rep and asked him what to do. The sales rep said he would be happy to provide training to all her employees, and to Sally herself. For Sally had realized she didn't really know what she was doing when it came to transactions.

The moral of the story is that merchants need make sure their cashiers know what they are doing. Mistakes can be very expensive in terms of money and customer retention.

Visa publishes a Point of Sale Reminder Card, specifically for cashiers. It's a simple brochure with three columns of information. The Reminder Card explains how to spot counterfeit cards, along with how to process a credit card sale. Swipe the card, enter the dollar amount, check the authorization response, then compare the signature on the card to the sales receipt. The cashier is advised to hold on to the card until the transaction is completed.

Unfortunately, most cashiers don't do it this way.

Many customers do not sign the back of their credit cards. They believe that signing the card is an invitation to fraud. Most merchants accept the card anyway. Neither the customers nor the merchants realize that an unsigned card is invalid, according to the card associations. What the merchants and the customers forget is that if the card is signed, and subsequently stolen and used fraudulently, the maximum amount the cardholder is liable for is only $50. Yet if the card is unsigned and used fraudulently, the cardholder's liability is unlimited.

An unsigned card can get very, very expensive for both the cardholder and the merchant.

In reality, unsigned cards are the invitation to fraud. If the unsigned card is stolen or the user is dishonest, an invalid card may result in an automatic Chargeback to the merchant. Any merchant who accepts unsigned cards is, in effect, giving away merchandise. In addition, any merchant who accepts an unsigned credit card violates his processing contract.

The card associations prohibit merchants from asking customers using credit cards for identification. Yet many cashiers still ask customers for identification, believing they are protecting everyone involved. Usually, the cashiers glance at the name on the proffered driver's license, checking to see if it matches the name on the credit card. Occasionally, the cashiers compare the photo on the driver's license with the person standing in front of them. If they resemble each other, the cashiers sincerely believe they have done their job.

The problem with checking identification is twofold. First, if cashiers took the time to properly review I.D.s, checking not just names and photos but also height, weight, eye color and hair color, the line of people waiting to pay for their groceries would stretch out the door into the parking lot.

Angry, impatient customers are not good for business.

The second problem is that cashiers do not have the training or expertise to spot counterfeit credit cards or fake I.D.s. Even trained professionals have difficulty in recognizing fake I.D.s, especially those of high quality, which can be very convincing.

Merchants should train cashiers never to accept unsigned credit cards. And to always, always, always compare the signature on the back of signed credit cards with the signature on the receipt. By and large, most cashiers do not compare the signatures. Failure to fulfill this simple procedure may result in the merchant losing thousands of dollars.

For example, Robert Smith goes into Best Buy and purchases a new laptop computer. The model he selects is top of the line with all the bells and whistles, the fastest processing chip available, and a massive hard-drive. When Mr. Smith arrives at the cashier to pay for his purchase, he pulls out his Visa card. The cashier takes the card, rings up the transaction, and then places the receipt on the counter to be signed.

Unfortunately, Robert Smith is dishonest. The card is his and it is valid. It even carries his signature on the back. Yet Mr. Smith dislikes paying for things. So he often goes into busy stores, such as Best Buy, and watches the cashiers. He watches to see if the cashiers routinely compare signatures or if they merely try to keep the line of customers moving as rapidly as possible. When he finds a store where the cashiers are easy-going and careless, he goes shopping.

On this occasion, Robert Smith has already determined that the cashiers at this particular Best Buy are indifferent. They don't normally compare signatures. So instead of signing the receipt Robert Smith, today he signs Ronald Sith. The cashier does not check the signatures. She simply smiles and says, "Have a nice day." Mr. Smith walks out with a brand new, top of the line, expensive laptop computer.

When he gets home, Mr. Smith calls Visa and contests the charge. Visa notifies the processor, who notifies Best Buy. Best Buy pulls the receipt. Because the cashier did not compare and verify the signatures, Best Buy has just given Mr. Smith a free computer. And Best Buy will get hit with a Chargeback.

Credit cards carry a three-digit security code on the back. Many online merchants request the three-digit security code from customers, when an order is placed. This request is acceptable. However, merchants are not allowed to record this security code in any manner. If the card associations discover that a merchant has recorded any security codes, the card association may impose a $100,000 to $500,000 fine for each violation.

Some retail establishments require cashiers to take imprints of credit cards, in addition to the card being swiped. This practice protects the merchant in cases where customers may dispute or may not remember making transactions. The problem is that some cashiers not only get an imprint of the card, they also write the customer's address on the imprint. This is strictly forbidden by the card associations, and if it occurs, will result in massive fines, sometimes as much as $1 million, depending on the circumstances.

The reason for the above exorbitant fines is simple. Identity theft occurs when thieves have access to four pieces of information: the three-digit security code, the credit card number, the expiration date, and the address associated with the card. Identity theft costs the card associations literally billions of dollars every year, and effectively devastates the personal finances of myriad individuals throughout the world.

Merchants who fail to properly protect customers' information may be liable in court, if the information is stolen or accidentally released for any reason.

Merchants who offer goods online need to train their personnel to verify shipping addresses or have an adequate address verification system in place. For example, Amazon requires customers to provide a billing address and a shipping address.

Online merchants must use Secure Socket Layer (SSL) protected systems. SSL pages have the image of a 'padlock' on the upper toolbar. If the 'padlock' image is not visible, both the customer and the merchant are at risk. On the customers' part, their credit card information is exposed and unprotected, which can result in identity theft. And any merchant who exposes his customers' credit card information is opening himself up to large fines and lawsuits.

Up until the recent Financial Regulations imposed by Congress, which went into effect in 2010, merchants could not set a minimum purchase level for customers to use a credit card. However, many merchants did just that. For instance, a coffee shop in Northern California refused to allow customers to use credit or debit cards on purchases less than $5. By setting a minimum level, the coffee shop was trying to save money on processing costs.

At the time, this minimum purchase requirement violated the clearly stated guidelines of the card associations, who told cardholders they could use their cards like cash.

Now, however, Congress has authorized merchants to set a minimum purchase level of $10. Any merchant that chooses to do so is not subject to Chargebacks or fines from processors or the card associations. Most merchants probably view the $10 minimum purchase level as a way to increase their profits. Yet because so few customers carry cash in today's world, thus relying on their credit and debit cards, implementing a $10 minimum may be disadvantageous for merchants. To put it simply, their customers may go somewhere else, someplace more convenient. For example, if the suits at Starbuck's corporate headquarters decided to implement the $10 minimum purchase level at Starbuck's outlets, there is no doubt business would drop off dramatically. People who go into Starbuck's for their morning cup of coffee or latte expect to be able to use their credit cards and debit cards. Part of what they are paying for is convenience, as well as ambiance and flavorful drinks.

Savvy merchants are advised to forgo the $10 minimum in the name of convenience and customer retention. They can still increase their profit margins by merely raising their prices by 1% across the board. This nominal increase will more than cover all their credit card fees.

Merchants who add a surcharge for credit card customers are in violation of the card associations' rules and guidelines. In short, the card associations do not allow such surcharges, which are little more than an attempt to discourage customers from using credit cards. Why? Because the merchant does not want to pay processing fees. According to Visa, merchants that accept credit cards increase sales by 56% over merchants that do not accept credit cards. Thus, it is in the best interests of any merchant to accept credit cards.

The card associations' guidelines do allow merchants to offer cash discounts. And under the 2010 Financial Regulations, merchants are now authorized to encourage customers to use certain types of credit cards. For example, merchants may put up a sign stating they prefer to accept MasterCard instead of American Express.

Merchants need to be on the lookout for "skimming devices." Skimming devices are handheld and record the information encrypted on the magnetic strip of credit cards. Thieves often pay cashiers to use the skimmers. The cashier swipes the card across the skimmer, and then swipes the card in the merchant's terminal to process the transaction. The first swipe records the card's information in the skimmer. Most customers don't think twice about the double-swipe.

Customers are most vulnerable to skimming in establishments where their card leaves their sight, such as restaurants. The waiter or waitress picks up the card and walks away to process the transaction. However, before the legitimate transaction is processed on the restaurant's terminal, the waitress swipes the card across a skimmer, which she carries in her apron.

Merchants should never process credit cards for another business. For example, two stores in a local mall. The first store, Barb's Beauty Supplies, does not accept credit cards. The second store, California Styling Salon, does accept credit cards. A customer walks into Barb's Beauty Supplies and buys three cases of expensive hair conditioner. The customer wants to pay with a credit card. Rather than lose a large sale, the cashier runs next door to California Styling Salon and asks them to ring up the sale. Since the salon does a lot of business with Barb's Beauty Supply, which gives the salon a discount, they process the transaction.

This practice is called 'factoring.' Factoring is when business A runs business B's transactions through business A's merchant processing account. Put simply, factoring is considered fraud, regardless of the circumstances or intentions.

Merchants need to make sure their cashiers understand the difference between 'voiding' a transaction and 'returns.' For example, an upscale men's clothing store has two processing accounts on one terminal. The store utilizes two accounts to increase its profit margin. One account is for Qualified, swiped, transactions, while the other account is for hand-keyed transactions, which are Mid-Qualified.

The sales clerk processes a $5,000 transaction, when in fact the number should have been $500. Realizing the mistake, the clerk processes a return for $5,000. When the owner of the men's store receives his next processing statement, he notices a $250 charged for the clerk's mistake.

Mistakes happen all the time. How they are handled is vital. In this case, the processor's computer recognized a $5,000 charge and a $5,000 return. As a result, the bank transferred $5,000 to the store's account and then back to the customer's account. In other words, the clerk inadvertently cost the employer $250. If the clerk had voided the transaction rather than performing a return, the fee would have been around $.50.

'Returns' move money around. 'Voiding' does exactly what the term means. It nullifies the transaction, and since no money is being moved the store is not charged a percentage of the sale.

The clerk's mistake was one of ignorance. The merchant failed to properly train his employee. Ultimately, the mistake can be attributed to the merchant.

Merchants should never use their own credit card in their store's terminal. Doing so is considered a cash advance. Credit card issuers allow cash advances, but such advances usually carry a 3 to 5% fee. When a merchant runs his card through his terminal, the card issuer receives only the Interchange fee.

This is fraud.

Many merchants are unaware that Chargebacks may be pursued up to three years after the transaction occurs. In other words, merchants must keep meticulous records. Failure to do so will, in the case of a Chargeback, result in the loss of the sale, unless pertinent information is available.

Merchants, especially online merchants with multiple websites, must be sure that the name of the business processing the transaction appears on the customer's credit card statement. If it does not, merchants run the risk of Chargebacks and factoring.

This brings up an interesting point about Chargebacks. Presumably, in the United States, individuals are considered innocent until proven guilty. This is not the case as far as Chargebacks are concerned. When it comes to Chargebacks, card issuers consider merchants guilty until they prove themselves innocent.

Card issuers initiate a Chargeback when a cardholder complains. Notification of the Chargeback is sent to the merchant. Once the merchant receives the Chargeback notification, he has a very small window of opportunity to provide proof that the transaction occurred. If the merchant misses the window of opportunity or fails to provide complete documentation of the transaction, he will be hit with the Chargeback.

Often, Chargebacks occur because merchants do not specify their return policy on receipts. If Sally's Candy Shoppe does not allow exchanges or refunds on purchased items, Sally's receipts must state the policy clearly. Neglecting to do so means that when a customer desires to exchange a box of candy, Sally has two options. She can make the exchange or she can risk a Chargeback.

Chapter 12
The Cost of Doing Business

The card associations, Visa, MasterCard, American Express and Discover, are in business to make money. And they do! They make billions of dollars every year off of swipe fees alone. The acquiring banks (merchants' banks) and the issuing banks (customers' banks) are also in business to make money. Most of their profit is generated from fees. The same holds true with processors and independent sales organizations (ISOs).

Making money is the name of the game.

Merchants want to make money. To do so, merchants must provide something customers want: goods or services. Customers also desire convenience, quality, expertise, and assistance when purchasing goods and services. Convenience is of primary importance to customers. And credit cards/debit cards are convenient. In other words, customers *want* to pay with credit cards. The customers' desire results in merchants choosing to accept credit cards in order to satisfy customers. In today's world, a merchant who does not accept credit cards will not be in business very long. If a merchant does not accept credit cards, customers will pay by cash, but only if the merchant sells goods or services the customers absolutely need and cannot purchase anywhere else. Otherwise, customers will not return to do business with a merchant who does not accept credit cards. The merchant who does not accept credit cards is cutting off his nose to spite his face.

In the end, when it comes to credit card fees, merchants have three options: first, merchants may refuse to accept credit cards. Refusal allows merchants to avoid any and all processing fees. The merchant's profit margin will automatically be higher if he is not paying innumerable fees. In fact, the merchant can lower prices across the board, allowing him to undercut his competitors.

Unfortunately, as outlined in the previous paragraphs, that won't happen. The merchant who thinks he can beat the system by refusing credit cards is deluded. Credit cards have become as normal as breathing. If the merchant stopped breathing he would drop dead. By the same token, if he stops accepting credit cards, financial death will be the rapid result.

Second, merchants may pass the cost of credit card processing, the price of convenience, to the customer. For example, if 50% of a merchant's customers utilize credit cards, the merchant simply adds 50% of his processing fees to the cost of his products. In other words, if the fee rate is 3%, the cost increase applied to each product is 1.5%. In this manner, the merchant circumvents the clause in his processing contract that states cardholders must not pay any additional cost for using credit cards.

Third, merchants may increase the price of all goods and services by a small percentage. For example, if a merchant raises all his prices by 5%, the increase will cover the fees associated with credit cards, plus a small profit margin. Since customers desire and expect to pay for quality, expertise, service, and convenience, merchants who actually provide legendary service attract more business.

In the final analysis, unless some cataclysmic, unforeseen transformation occurs in the world of commerce, credit/debit cards are here to stay. The cards may assume a different form, becoming a tab or coded bar on the back of a cell phone, but what they represent, convenience, remains. And convenience is accompanied by processing fees. To put it simply, credit card fees are here to stay.

For merchants, in the contemporary world, the cost of doing business includes paying credit card fees. No alternative exists.

Made in the USA
Monee, IL
19 July 2026

57615188R10069